Cross Country Riding

Cross Country Riding

Edited by Michael Clayton

E.P. Dutton New York

Title page
Racing at Newton Abbot

Copyright © Walter Parrish International Limited 1977

All rights reserved.

First American edition published 1977 by E. P. Dutton, a Division
of Sequoia-Elsevier Publishing Company, Inc., New York.

Produced by Walter Parrish International Limited, London
Designed by Harry Green

Printed and bound in Great Britain by Purnell & Sons Ltd

Library of Congress Catalog Card Number: 77-77956
ISBN: 0-87690-254-9

Contents

Introduction

'Spread out' is the cry. It is one of the most exciting exhortations in the hunting field. For it is the signal from the Field Master that the fences ahead are jumpable along a broad front. No need to queue—the horsemen can attack the obstacle ahead as it comes. For some there is a thorn hedge, but here and there it has been patched with timber rails. A broad ditch lurks on the landing side. The first group of horses gallops on and clears timber or hedge, landing well out over the ditch beyond. A thrilling crack, crack, as horses brush through the top growth of the hedge, then a second rank follows, and a succeeding ruck of horses jumps more raggedly; here and there a refusal; and on the landing side some horses peck, or land in the wide ditch beyond.

Soon riderless horses are galloping among those after the leaders. Their unseated riders, bruised at least and rueful, struggle across the grass in pursuit on foot. There is no person more obviously disorientated than the horseman unseated in a cross country ride. Unless he can retain his horse and remount immediately, the fallen rider is out of the hunt if the pace is sharp.

But there is some relief in being able to walk at all; this is a risk sport, and a fall can occasionally bring pain and even permanent injury. Head, neck and back are the dangerously vulnerable parts when being catapulted from a falling horse; after that there is still the risk of an inadvertent kick from your own horse or, worst of all, a following horse landing on you. See how professional jockeys lie curled in a ball when they have fallen to give following horses the utmost chance to avoid them.

Why take the risks? Why do more people than ever before seek to take chances which involve the ultimate penalties of paralysis or fatal injury?

The truth is there is no other thrill to compare with riding a high-couraged horse across fences at speed. The challenge is manifest; the demands on a rider's nerve are clear; the tests of skill are less easy to define; but the pleasures and thrills of cross country riding are compounded of many other elements.

Certainly, the partnership between horse and rider in taking on a challenge where they both risk their necks, and the sheer variety of problems which occur in a cross country ride, make the sport one which captures enthusiasts for a lifetime.

I refer to *a* sport, but there is nowadays a host of cross country sports emanating from the original challenge of riding over fences across grass in trying to keep as near as possible to a pack of hounds hunting their fox. The original still exists, and flourishes, but the varied riches which the hunting field has produced for the entire equestrian world are immense.

Hunting is, of course, one of man's oldest activities, and hunting for sport as well as food goes back well beyond recorded history. In Britain, hunting was influenced dramatically by '1066 and all that'. William the Conqueror brought organization to the hunting-field, just as he did to so many other aspects of life in England. The Normans brought science as well as enthusiasm to the chase in the great forests. The notes of the horn, and the language of the huntsman in charge of hounds, became more formalized, and so did the procedures of the chase.

'Tally ho', the most famous English hunting cry, came from the Norman hunting vocabulary—'Ty a hillaut' was the warning that a deer had roused himself. The deer was the quarry in the sport of kings for centuries, and it must be remembered that hunting had that title long before racing was evolved.

Foxhunting was a third-rate sport compared with staghunting until the 18th century, when the great forests began to give way to more pasture and arable land, as farming methods became more ambitious. There had been plenty of galloping in pursuit of staghounds, but such jumping as occurred in the chase tended to be over ditches or natural banks, since land enclosed by fences scarcely existed, and did not have to be crossed during a hunt.

'Craning' was the order of the day when foxhunting began to increase in popularity in the early 18th century. This meant a rider stopping to crane over an obstacle to see what lay on the other side, and if a vertical jump was required then it would probably be performed from a trot or a standstill.

The Duke of Beaufort's Hunt in 1762 perfectly illustrates why sportsmen began to change their allegiance from staghunting to foxhunting. The 5th Duke when a young man was passing Silk Wood on his way home after a poor day's sport and threw his hounds into a covert; a fox was found which gallantly faced the open; a capital hunt was the result. According to the sporting writer Cecil, this 'so delighted the young sportsman that the Badminton hounds were forthwith steadied from deer and encouraged to fox'.

But it was the great grazing grounds of Leicestershire which saw the most intense form of riding to foxhounds. Enclosure of the immense acres of pasture land there produced fields bordered by the new thorn hedges. In the summer time, bullocks maddened by flies tended to smash the hedges down, so they were often guarded by rails, hence the 'oxer' and, with rails on both sides of a hedge, the 'double oxer'—a formidable jump indeed when the rails stood far out.

One obstacle did not exist—the curse of barbed wire. It only remained for foxhunters to develop horses capable of jumping the hedges and the rails.

Much of the credit for introducing a style of riding which defeated those Leicestershire fences is given to a Shropshire man, William Childe, or 'Flying Childe' as he was known. He was a natural horseman with unbreakable nerve, great strength and the natural talent to keep a horse balanced and going well no matter what the gradient, no matter how large the obstacle.

Childe used to horrify the locals in Shropshire by galloping down the steepest slopes on the Clee Hills. When he came to Leicestershire, the great Hugo Meynell was Master of the Quorn Hunt, and he did not exactly welcome Childe's introduction of speed into the hunting-field since it increased the chance of his hounds being over-ridden. Meynell complained that he 'had not enjoyed a day's happiness since they developed their racing ideas'.

But riding to hounds with zest and speed had come to stay. The practice grew up of bringing a second horse to the hunting-field; horses were then better conditioned for galloping and jumping. The Meltonians, those based at Melton Mowbray, set the fashion, and John Moore memorably paid tribute to them in his foreword to Nimrod's *Life of a Sportsman*:

'They were polished and tough, cruel and elegant, brave as lions and thoughtless as butterflies, these foxhunting gentry with their spindly legs and their queer, peaky faces peering out between the absurd high collars up to their ears . . . The Meltonians had a million faults, among which you may or may not include their absolute monomania for breaking their necks. They were as wanton as weeds, ungoverned wild weeds strangely blossoming in the ordered fields of our history. They were selfish, drunken, socially useless if you like; but when they were asked how in God's name they managed to get across those huge breakneck ox-fences they answered gaily: "We send our hearts over first, and then follow them in the best way we can." And I, for one, can forgive them anything for that.'

In the 18th century the Irish gentry were inclined to vie with each other in 'pounding matches'. A leader, decided by taking lots, would choose as stiff a course across country as he dared. His competitor would follow or lose by default, and the winner was he who 'pounded' his opponent to a standstill. It was a highly dangerous sport, causing some grievous injuries, and some sort of rules were eventually formed whereby such rides were held over an agreed route, using a church steeple as a landmark to the winning post; hence steeplechasing.

As the enclosure of Leicestershire changed foxhunting in the late 18th and early 19th centuries, the growth of steeplechase matches among the young bloods of England became inevitable.

They were now using thoroughbred sires to produce hunters which could readily gallop and jump and, although following hounds was the priority, it was inevitable that private wagers about a horse's prowess led to informal cross country contests. Enormous sums were wagered on the outcome of these races. It is recorded that the first time steeplechase riders wore colours was in a race in November 1804, when three gentlemen raced from Wornack's Lodge to Woodwell, a line of some eight miles.

Not all foxhunters approved of steeplechasing. Nimrod, the great foxhunting correspondent, described it as a 'cocktail sport', and with others condemned it as being unnecessarily cruel to horses. One foxhunting man pointed out: 'In the chase the little checks that occur give relief to the animal and afford him the opportunity of recovering his wind. Not so in the steeplechase. There a distance of four or five miles is selected, over which the poor beast is ridden at the top of his speed and without a chance of regaining his wind, except by happening to fail at a leap over which his distressed condition was not equal to carry him.'

Such problems, and the need for spectators to be able to see more of the action, led to more formalized steeplechasing, with the St Albans Steeplechase in 1830 being the first to establish itself as a popular annual meeting. Seven years later the first Grand National took place and steeplechasing's development as a major national winter sport was on its way. It was to be a sport emulated abroad as well, but not surprisingly it has developed most successfully in countries where foxhunting also flourished. The history of organized steeplechasing in Ireland has run parallel to that in England, and in the United States the tradition of steeplechasing followed the development of foxhunting.

Virginia and Pennsylvania saw the formation of hunts in the late 18th century and 19th century run broadly on English lines, and many other packs followed after the turn of the century. The natural terrain and the development of agriculture in America did not usually provide thorn hedges, but timber rails were easier to find. English foxhunters visiting the United States and hunting there for the first time are often surprised by the size and solidity of the timber jumped as a matter of course by American foxhunters, especially in Virginia and Maryland.

In return, the American foxhunter abroad is drawn to the fresh challenge of England's fly fences, or the wildness of Ireland's banks and ditches. Although much of the tradition of American cross country riding was inevitably linked to the cow pony roaming the plains, there is a separate history of riding fences at speed in those eastern and southern States where farming developed on enclosed land.

American owners have a long history of active interest in steeplechasing in Britain as well as at home. It was in 1922 that an American, Mr Stephen Sandford, bought a horse called Sergeant Murphy and won the Grand National at Aintree with him the following year. Three years later, the great race was won by Jack Horner, owned by an American, Mr A. C. Schwartz.

But the most famous link between the American hunting and racing tradition and that of the United Kingdom, from which it originally sprang through the sporting instincts of 'Southern gen'lemen', was the victory of Jay Trump in the Grand National of 1965.

This superb 'chaser, owned by Mrs M. Stephenson, had won America's famous Maryland Hunt Cup, a race across solid timber which would cause more than a little apprehension in the breast of even the most experienced English 'chasing jockey.

Note how the tradition of racing springs from the hunting field, for in America timber racing is a long-established sport, whereas it has never been practised under rules in England. Hitting a solid timber fence at speed is indeed a formidable prospect. Mr Tommy Crompton Smith had won the Maryland with Jay Trump, but riding the thorn fences and big drops of Aintree on the same horse was a different sort of challenge.

Trained by Fred Winter, Jay Trump and Smith proved they could triumph over the unique hazards of the National course just as effectively as over their fearsome timber at home.

One tradition of racing over fences which is peculiarly English and Irish, and flourishes today more than ever before, is point-to-point racing, which retains the closest link of all with the hunting field, since horses have to be qualified by appearing out with hounds earlier in the winter.

Hunt racing dates from early in the last century, and from February to May it captures sizeable crowds of spectators at meetings run by each of the 200 or so packs of foxhounds eligible to run races under Jockey Club rules. Here, the young man or woman who has first thrilled to the excitement of jumping fences when following hounds, may don silk for the first time and take on the challenge of the Members' Race, open only to subscribers of the hunt running the meeting.

Cross country has now taken on a new meaning in international equestrianism, since it is the vital phase of combined training or horse trials. Combined training did not spring directly from the hunting field. Its origins are strictly military, mainly on the continent of Europe. The French held the first real forerunner of the modern Three Day Event, with their *Championnat du Cheval d'Armes*, held by their cavalry near Paris in April 1902.

The three phases of combined training are of course dressage, cross country, and showjumping, of which the cross country is the most influential on the final result. Probably because of their absorption with hunting and racing, British, Irish and American horsemen shone but little in eventing in pre-war years, although it was established as an Olympic sport in 1912.

Even today, the English in particular do not excel in pure international dressage at its highest levels because too few of its leading riders choose this form of riding for specialization, since they have so many other opportunities. The farmer's son or daughter who learns to ride as soon as walk is far more likely to become a local point-to-point champion than to take up the more technical, less exciting disciplines of pure dressage.

Combined training, however, demands only basic dressage and offers the thrill of a really tough cross country ride. Its postwar growth coincided with a boom in riding as a recreational attraction throughout Western countries, and when Princess Anne chose it as her special riding sport the popularity of combined riding was assured throughout the United Kingdom.

The Duke of Beaufort, Master of the Queen's Horse, and the longest serving and most distinguished Master of Foxhounds, has done enormous service to the sport by inaugurating Badminton Three Day Event on his Gloucestershire estate in 1949, since when it has become the premier horse trials in the fixture list.

The Burghley Three Day Event in the autumn is the other key feature of the extensive British programme of eventing. Three times British teams have brought home gold medals from postwar Olympic Games; from Stockholm in 1956; Mexico in 1968 and Munich in 1972. Richard Meade is a triple gold medallist, having shared in the team triumphs in Mexico and Munich, and at the latter winning the individual gold as well.

America's growing reputation in international trials was proved with a vengeance in 1974 when Bruce Davidson came to Burghley from the States and snatched the world championship from Britain, the previous holders being Mary Gordon-Watson and the great Cornishman.

Davidson's triumph, and the establishment of America's Ledyard Farm Three Day Event, emphasize the extent of the growing challenge to British supremacy in eventing. The West Germans, already so successful in international showjumping, have been making special efforts at their training centre at Warendorf to improve their eventing prospects.

The Russians have already achieved much in this field, and are determined to do better, so that international competition in this tough sport is constantly sharpening.

Cross country riding takes other forms which attract thousands of competitors, and delight millions of spectators. Certainly, showjumping is a derivation in specialized form of cross country riding, but we need not press this case, for cross country riding in an'exceedingly natural format has found a new television audience in Great Britain, and has set off a brand new sport.

Douglas Bunn, who owns and runs the All England Jumping Course at Hickstead, is a keen hunting man who rides to hounds regularly in Leicestershire and is Joint Master of his local pack of draghounds, the Mid-Surrey, who perform over hair-raising lines of big fences south of the Thames.

In 1974 he held the first Team Cross Country Ride at Hickstead, with full BBC television coverage. It was an instant success with viewers and competitors. He had teams of soldiers, foxhunters, jockeys, dressage riders, showjumpers and many others, riding a stiff course of large thorn hedges and ditches. There were four in a team; three had to finish and the time of the last of the three across the finishing line was the time achieved by the team. It is a formula which avoids the accusation that it is simply a race, but it provides the thrills of seeing horses tackling big fences abreast, and fallers are able to remount and carry on.

Imitators sprang up quickly all over Britain, following a similar formula. Princess Anne and Capt. Mark Phillips took part in a Team Ride organized by the Pytchley Hunt in Northamptonshire. Already there is a long fixture list of such rides from the North Riding of Yorkshire down to the South-west.

Some members of the horse world are perturbed, since there is as yet no overall code of rules for these rides and some fear their popularity may threaten other horse sports. As yet, there is no sign of this, but the story of cross country riding may well have taken a new turn—a turn not so far removed from its inceptions in the hunting field—and who is to say that this would be a bad thing?

This book is divided into three main sections, covering hunting, steeplechasing and eventing, and within each there are chapters dealing with the sport in Britain, America and continental Europe. There is an extra chapter in the steeplechasing section on point-to-pointing and Team Cross Country in Britain.

The contributors write from their various individual viewpoints, however, and no attempt has been made to impose over-rigid guidelines relating to coverage or style. At the beginning of each section there is a brief resumé of basic information about the sport to which it relates.

Three chapters fall outside the scheme described above. Philip Blacker, a current British steeplechase jockey with a distinguished equestrian background, contributes a personal account of a 'chasing visit to America. Chris Collins gives a most apposite account of his own experiences in coming to eventing from a background in amateur steeplechasing. The last chapter in the book, by the celebrated Director and course-designer at Badminton, Colonel Frank Weldon, gives practical advice on the choice and training of a cross country horse which will be particularly valuable to anyone wanting to make a start in cross country riding in any of its various forms.

HUNTING

Hunting is probably the oldest of sports. All other branches of cross country riding derive from riding to hounds.

Foxhunting is the most popular form of hunting in Britain, with about 200 packs flourishing. There are more than 25 in Ireland, 140 in the United States, and about a dozen in Canada. Foxhunting in Britain, Ireland and America is strictly administered by Masters of Foxhounds Associations.

Harrier packs, which mainly hunt hares, but may also hunt the fox in some cases, also provide considerable sport for mounted followers, but have declined in numbers in Britain where there are now only about 26, and the same number in Ireland.

Drag hunting, the following of an artificially laid scent by a pack of hounds, has a very small following in England, and can be found elsewhere in the world where foxhunting is impractical or impossible.

The spread of rabies in foxes has rendered normal foxhunting impossible on the continent of Europe, but deerhunting, boar and hare hunting abound in France where there are about 120 packs of all types.

Riding to Hounds in Britain and Ireland

Michael Clayton

Hunting men, like all enthusiasts, disagree on many aspects of their sport—the best conditions for holding scent, the most effective hound-breeding policy, the right way to tie a stock . . .

But there is one thing with which all will sadly concur: riding to hounds in Britain and Ireland is not what it was.

The reasons are manifest: the postwar change in British farming methods meant an enormous change from pasture to plough in most areas, the increasing urbanization of the countryside brought more roads and heavier traffic, and there are far more built-up areas in previously remote districts.

All these factors obviously reduce the possibilities of galloping on grass, taking fly fences as they come, swooping along on the flank of a flying pack of hounds . . . all the ingredients of the chase at its most exhilarating.

Yet before we mourn the passage of time too deeply, it must be pointed out that more people hunt in the United Kingdom than ever before. Hunting in the Irish Republic still flourishes, and in the United States, Canada, Australia and New Zealand, there are many ardent riders to hounds—whether those hounds are pursuing red foxes or grey foxes, or chasing a hare, or simply following a drag line. The heroosh of the chase still exerts a powerful spell, and there are plenty of opportunities for young people to ride over natural country following hounds. Although the terrain has changed considerably, the challenge is still there—and so are the rewards.

Nowadays, it is increasingly difficult to visit a great number of hunts. Before World War II, many a young Army officer saw hunting with many packs through being posted to different areas of Britain. There was a far greater availability of Army horses, hirelings were generally to be found in most districts, and most hunts were able to welcome visitors.

Spare horses are now much more difficult, if not impossible to find in modern Britain; few stables find it economic to hire out hunters; and the hunts themselves are hard pressed to accommodate those living within their boundaries and are reluctant to risk upsetting local farming interests by allowing their mounted fields to be swollen with unlimited visitors.

Opposite
North Shropshire Hunt: Mrs Robin Thompson, wife of the Joint Master, clearing a tiger trap

Thus limits on the numbers of visitors are common, and finding a suitable horse locally is almost out of the question for the visitor.

The Melton Hunt Club performs a wonderful service to young foxhunters in arranging visiting days with the famous Shire packs, on a ticket basis. In return, the Club provides a sizeable contribution to the hunts' costs in maintaining fences and taking down barbed wire during the hunting season.

As a hunting correspondent, I have been extremely fortunate in visiting packs of hounds all over Britain and Ireland, often being very well mounted and having an opportunity to see hounds hunting in some of their best pieces of country. In my view, this privilege imposes a duty to range as far and wide as possible, by no means frequenting only the 'fashionable' counties, and this has been a rewarding and worthwhile policy.

In recent years I have been hunting with as many as 42 packs each season, riding as many as 50 different horses, and it has been a wonderful opportunity to explore the hunting field in so many widely varying settings.

The greatest surprise in life is surely to be surprised by joy, and this I have experienced more frequently in the hunting field than anywhere else in the world. A quiet day will suddenly explode into the stern excitements of a quick run across daunting fences or ditches; an ascent of a hilltop suddenly reveals a view of throat-catching beauty; a jog home will reveal hounds and huntsman on the breast of a slope, against the background of a glorious sunset.

What sort of perspectives are to be seen, what variety of challenges is still available in riding to hounds through the length and breadth of Britain and Ireland? Come with me . . .

There are some 204 packs of foxhounds listed in Britain (compared with 177 in 1905) and 33 in Ireland (24 in 1905). Harrier packs, also followed on horseback, have decreased: 26 in the United Kingdom now, compared with 101 in 1905; 25 in Ireland (39 in 1905).

Staghounds have decreased, there being now only four packs in England (16 in 1905); and two in Ireland (four in 1905).

Draghounds, packs which follow an artificial line of scent laid by man, increased between the wars, but nowadays number only nine in Britain, the same number as were listed in 1905. None are listed in Ireland, although I know of a Harrier Master who will openly hunt a drag line at the beginning of the day 'just to warm things up' before his hounds are allowed to hunt fox, hare or even deer.

Baily's Hunting Directory, which provides the above figures, lists altogether some 443 packs of all kinds in Great Britain and Ireland, compared with 392 in 1905, so there is nowadays more hunting available, even if the countryside has shrunk in so many areas of England. Beagles, bassets, and otterhounds are followed on foot of course, but there are four packs of bloodhounds which are followed on horseback, and hunt 'clean boot', the scent of a man who if he is 'caught' is guaranteed to receive no more than a friendly lick on the face.

Opposite
The Warwickshire Hunt with their huntsman Clarence Webster out cub-hunting in the early morning

The Exmoor Hunt has one of
the best moorland countries in
Britain. A hunt in April 1977.

The West Country

Hunting in every pack has a distinctive character, but the West Country is particularly
strong in local colour, both in the setting and the sporting people you will meet.

Cornwall has five packs of foxhounds, and still offers the challenge of jumping
banks; there are some stone walls; some arable, but plenty of grass and moorland as well.

The West and South-west of England is a big stock-rearing area, so for the cross
country rider the worst hazard is inevitably barbed wire.

Devon has 17 packs of foxhounds, plus two packs of harriers, and the famous packs
of staghounds on Exmoor, the Devon and Somerset, and the Tiverton.

It is on the moors that you will find the most crossable country in Devon, and the
two moorland areas, Exmoor and Dartmoor, have totally distinctive features. Exmoor is
easier to ride, in my experience. The spring and autumn staghunting offers wonderful
gallops across grass and springy heather. There is little or no jumping, but this does not
mean that there is no hazard or excitement in crossing this country fast.

There are steep-sided valleys, or coombes, where deer are often found, and the
Devon and Somerset followers will gallop down the steep sides at a daunting pace.
Patches of bog have to be avoided on the open moorland, and good horsemanship is
essential in saving your horse and crossing the country during long days.

The red deer of Exmoor can provide far longer hunts than are usually achieved in
foxhunting. Points of more than 10 miles are more frequent, although in recent years

Opposite
The opening meet of the
Warrenton Hunt in Virginia,
with huntsman Fred Duncan in
the foreground

the deer are not so likely to make such distances. As Exmoor becomes an increasingly busy holiday centre, the deer become far more used to noise and disturbance and are more difficult to rouse from the dense woods and coverts which clothe the coombes.

However, I have enjoyed some magnificent runs of as many as 14 miles. With the blue of the Bristol Channel often on the horizon, and the greens, browns and purples of the moorland and grass under your horse's feet, a gallop across Exmoor behind the staghounds is an unforgettable experience.

We are more concerned with the ride across country than the science of venery in this book, but it must be said that it is the staghounds which cull the red deer of Exmoor effectively, and ensure that they are not killed haphazardly by poachers which would soon exterminate the species altogether. This nearly happened during a period when the staghounds ceased to function.

The deer is always despatched with a gun at close quarters at the end of a run, an infinitely more merciful end than random attempts at shooting from longer range by shotgun, or by snaring or poisoning.

I have had great fun hunting on Dartmoor where the granite tors are not the only evidence of the rocky core of this great, wild moorland. There are slabs and fragments of rock among much of the gorse and heather, and your horse must be surefooted and clever to cross these surfaces at speed. A fall on the rocks can be, in Jorrocks's words, 'a h'awful thing' indeed.

The moor has some fearsome bogs, and Major Michael Howard, Master and huntsman of the Spooner's and West Dartmoor, tells me the fog can come so quickly that on occasions he has had to go home without his hounds.

Below
An anonymous hunt in full cry in the park of a stately home. A drawing by Randolph Caldecott illustrating his short story 'Mr Carlyon's Christmas' (1881).

'If they run hard down wind and the fog sets in, it is sometimes very difficult to get in touch with the pack, but they always find their way home eventually,' he said.

A contrasting day, in bright sunshine, was in the neighbouring South Devon country; they also hunt the moor, around the famous village of Widecombe ('w' Bill Brewer, Jan Stewer, Peter Gurney etc . . .').

One of the great hunting personalities of the West Country, Mr Claude Whitley, has been Master and huntsman of the South Devon since 1938, and I have enjoyed some grand days with Claude and his Joint Master, Denis Ferens, who also hunts the hounds nowadays. A day I particularly recall was during one of Ronnie Wallace's famous springtime tours of the West Country with the Heythrop hounds. There was a closely observant gallery of Masters and huntsmen as the Heythrop hounds set out to find a fox on a sparkling, sunny day when there seemed to be little or no scent.

'That's no way to find a fox,' said one local Master as Ronnie eventually dismounted to walk with his hounds through some very thick gorse. But find a fox they did, and hounds went away beautifully from Honeybag Tor, running to Hedgebarton Newtake, over Ruddycleave Mire to Buckland Beacon and on to Halshanger Mire; a four-mile point at a good pace before hounds marked their fox to ground.

Those Dartmoor granite slabs and ruts made the gallops anything but easy, but there were some stretches where we could really put on speed, an exhilarating experience on moorland where farm gates and wired-up fences do not pose the problems which can so easily arise on farmland.

Going east, Somerset offers some of the most entertaining hunting country anywhere. The Taunton Vale's Friday country is a very nice piece of grassland, with fly fences and timber to be jumped, and I have had great fun there.

The northern end of the Blackmore and Sparkford Vale country lies in Somerset. I would classify this hunt as having one of the half-dozen best countries in England, from a riding point of view. Crossing the Blackmore Vale, at the Dorset end, is a particularly daunting prospect if you are not well mounted. In the last century, the famous hunting correspondent Nimrod remarked: 'If any country in England requires a double set of eyes in men and horses it is the Vale of Blackmore.'

He was referring to the hedges being set on small banks. At one time it was possible to jump onto the banks, but the growth has become so thick that they must usually be jumped clear nowadays. There is always a ditch, which may be deep and wide, and frequently a drop landing. The hedge growth is often hairy and uninviting, altogether a severe test of boldness in horse and rider.

I was fortunate to be brought up in Dorset, and I hunted for some years with the neighbouring Portman country which has a slice of the vale from Shaftesbury down south of Sturminster Newton. This is still virtually all grass. Intensification of cattle-farming in the Dorset vales has made the problem of wire more prevalent in recent years.

But the Blackmore Vale, Portman, Cattistock, Seavington and South Dorset all have portions of vale which are thrilling to ride. It is no good popping these fences; your horse will all too easily land in a ditch on the landing side. The spreads are often disconcertingly wider than you first estimated, and the growth of the hedges is often so strong that a horse cannot easily brush through.

Of course, it is possible to find a way across these vales through the gateways, but

An example of the old-fashioned hunting seat.
Horse and rider coming off a stone-faced bank in
County Down, Northern Ireland.

the horse and rider who take on these fences boldly and successfully will have little or no difficulty in jumping any country in Britain. The enclosures tend to be small, and very large mounted fields—of the order of Leicestershire's—cannot be accommodated. The going, although grass, rides extremely deep in a normal season, and it is not therefore a real galloping country, but it is one of the most delightful and challenging areas to follow hounds that you could find anywhere.

Just to the north, the South and West Wilts has a nice piece of vale, and a great area of downland as well, much wired, but furnished with hunt rails to jump.

The South and South-east

'Get your hair cut once a week and never hunt south of the Thames,' was said to be a hunting man's advice to his son.

Hampshire has the unique New Forest which I strongly recommend as an interesting ride, and a fascinating setting in which to follow hounds. It is the nearest thing to a Norman forest still in existence: grassy glades where ponies and cattle graze, areas of thick forest, and best of all large areas of open heather and gorse, especially on the north side.

I have had some splendid hunting here with Sir Newton Rycroft's New Forest foxhounds, a remarkable pack which he has bred with originality and skill, using Welsh and French blood in his hounds. Again, there is nothing to jump, but some exciting gallops indeed in the open and hazardous going at times in the woodland rides, with hounds running among the trees, their cry echoing as if in a cathedral.

The fallow buck is still hunted here, as in Norman times, with the New Forest Buckhounds providing exciting runs in this one-time playground of William the Conqueror.

North Hampshire has long been condemned as a difficult scenting area, with large woodland areas, and nowadays lots of wire. But the H.H. (Hampshire Hunt) and the Hambledon overcome these difficulties to provide a lot of fun.

There is no denying that South-east England is extraordinarily well provided with hunts, yet particularly hard pressed for rideable country. Railway-lines, roads, and urban sprawl make Surrey, Kent and Sussex, and the counties bordering north, west and east London, hardly the ideal setting for the chase.

But I have had wonderful fun less than 30 miles from the heart of London. I used to hunt regularly with the Old Surrey and Burstow, and their marvellous huntsman, Jack Champion, managed to provide a lot of fun at Godstone, which is not far south of Croydon, or at Lingfield, or Edenbridge, all within easy drive of Piccadilly Circus.

One of the most frequent obstacles in the South-east is the 'tiger trap', the invention of which is generally attributed to the late Arthur Dalgetty when he had the Southdown. A triangular contraption of timber, it can be placed in a gap in any sort of fence or hedge, and may straddle a ditch or a small bank. It offers a reasonable obstacle which a horse will usually jump well; it can be constructed easily, and will last a long time if strong timber is used.

But even a tiger trap has its hazards. I have seen a horse slip on take off, slide into this timber triangle over a ditch and become hopelessly entangled, with great risk of kicking and crushing the rider who was somewhere underneath. It took us an hour's work with a large saw to free both of them, and yet they emerged with no lasting damage.

It says much for the lure of foxhunting that all the South-east packs are extremely well supported, including the Enfield Chase which probably hunts the most urban country of all, just north of London.

The most exciting ride in the South-east is undoubtedly provided by the Mid-Surrey Draghounds, a well established pack, presided over since the war with immense dash and flair by the Hon. Philip Kindersley.

Members ride selected drag lines in Kent, Surrey and Sussex, co-operating closely with the local hunts. I have had some thrilling rides indeed, for if you can pick your fences and remove the wire beforehand, this area provides some extraordinarily varied and formidable fly fences and timber, with plenty of grass.

East Anglia

'I am sorry there is not much to jump here; it's not very exciting,' said my host when I first visited a hunt in one of the Eastern counties.

Below
A pack which hunts in the plough areas of Eastern England: the Essex hounds on their way to a draw

He was very much understating the case, as I discovered when I came to my first Essex ditch: a chasm, it seemed, and it had to be jumped from one bank of slippery plough to another.

The secret of ditch-jumping anywhere is to walk to the edge, get forward, and kick on, giving your horse plenty of rein. You must get your weight off his back because if the ditch is really wide, your horse may only be able to land on the opposite slope and will need to throw his weight forward in scrambling up to the lip of the landing side. Sometimes it is necessary to slither part of the way down the take-off side, and then launch across the gap to the slope on the other side. It is amazing how horses can manage such leaps even when the sides of a ditch are nearly vertical, but they must not be interfered with by a nervous rider grabbing them by the head at a crucial moment, or leaning back.

Ireland is the place for the biggest ditch-jumping, but wherever it is encountered, it can evoke more than a few qualms at first in the breast of a rider who has hitherto only jumped vertical obstacles.

The worst error is to attempt to gallop on at wide ditches, as an unsound take-off cannot be detected in time, and a really crumpling fall into the ditch may follow.

Horses have an extraordinary capacity for feeling their way with their leading foot; camera shots show that they land on one foot; at the take-off side of a deep ditch I have many times been aware of a horse 'hovering' for a second or two as one foot feels for a sound place to push off as he launches himself at the far side.

Of course, falls will occur in ditches, but it is seldom that they are at all serious for the rider. It is speed that kills, and if they take it slowly a horse and rider can escape mishaps in open ditches and emerge without a scratch. It is when a horse jumps a hedge fast and lands heavily in a deep ditch that he is more likely to break his back.

I have ridden with a number of Eastern England packs, including the Essex, Puckeridge and Thurlow, Duston Harriers and Suffolk foxhounds.

Here are great countries for seeing a hunt; there is very little grass indeed, but seldom are you held up by wire. Riding fast over plough is an art in itself. The man who allows a horse to gallop in an uncollected fashion across deep, sticky plough is asking for trouble: sprained tendons or pulled muscles which may keep his horse at home for the rest of the season.

It was much easier when ploughing took the form of furrows, but the new rotary ploughs do not leave the convenient furrow which a horse can follow. Nowadays there is all too often a sea of loose, cultivated soil, stretching ahead for 30 acres or more. Far better on these occasions to choose a route round the edge of the field; with modern methods of drilling seeds it is all the more difficult to know whether a field has been sown, so you are far less likely to risk damage if you choose the edge.

Yet I have found many useful paths between the great, brown arable tracts of East Anglia, where a horse may gallop on sound going, and it is surprising what fast hunts can be enjoyed. With some really wide ditches en route, you will certainly experience thrills in this form of cross country riding, and you will probably see more of hounds than in a hedge country.

The South and West Midlands

The counties of Gloucestershire, Oxfordshire, Buckinghamshire, Berkshire and Warwickshire contain some of the most illustrious hunts, and some of the most enjoyable hunting areas in the world.

The Duke of Beaufort's country in Gloucestershire, and its neighbour the Heythrop, which straddles the Cotswold Hills into Oxfordshire, were once all one country. The huntsmen and whippers-in of both packs still wear the traditional green of the Beaufort pack, deriving from its staghunting past. But the Beaufort field is unique because hunt members wear the smart blue Beaufort livery, with buff facings. The visitor wearing a red coat really stands out, and any mistakes or misdemeanours he may make are only too detectable. The M4 motorway carved a damaging swathe through the Beaufort country, but it is still a remarkable area in which to follow hounds. The terrain varies from grass vales to upland with stone walls, and there is a marvellous hill country for spring and autumn hunting.

There is no more dedicated and gifted foxhunter than the 10th Duke of Beaufort who hunted his hounds himself for 47 years, and in his 77th year continues to ride hounds regularly with a professional huntsman, Brian Gupwell, nowadays carrying the horn. The Duke of Beaufort is a wonderfully generous host, and many a young

Above
Cutting out the work in High Leicestershire: Joint Master of the Quorn, Mr James Teacher, and some of the mounted field

foxhunter from the South-west has been invited to hunt with Master, as he is known to one and all in the hunting world.

The Beaufort country provides many a young foxhunter with a first taste of hunting 'on the grand scale'. The coverts are beautifully sited and maintained, the traditions of hunting are properly observed, and you need a quality horse to stay near hounds when they are running hard. The fences are not necessarily the largest you will encounter in a foxhunting tour, but they vary enormously and if you ride straight you will find yourself jumping some extremely formidable obstacles at times. The land on the hills rides fairly light, and although there is quite a lot of arable nowadays, it is much easier to cross than the heavy plough of East Anglia. In the vales the thorn grows strongly, and you need a sound performer who can jump cleanly and gallop on.

Undoubtedly riding in a large mounted field across huge enclosures is, as we'll see in looking at the Shires, a totally different prospect from following hounds across a less open country with a small band of followers.

North of the Beaufort country, alongside the River Severn, is one of the most interesting and formidable cross country terrains anywhere in Britain. This is the Berkeley country, with its reclaimed marshland by the river below Berkeley Castle, home of the senior Joint Master. He is Major John Berkeley, continuing a family tradition of hunting these hounds, deriving from the 16th and 17th centuries when the Earls of Berkeley hunted the country all the way from London to Bristol.

The distinctive feature of the modern Berkeley country is the reens or rhines, open ditches filled to the brink, and steep-sided. If a horse slips in, all too often the rider has to swim, and a tractor is needed to extract the horse.

There are also very deep and broad ditches lying by the thick thorn hedges, making a formidable jump which can only be tackled safely by really bold horses. The horse which hesitates loses impulsion and all too easily crashes into the ditch on the landing side. Unlike Ireland, there is every reason for taking these Berkeley obstacles at a good, strong pace, but the horse needs to be well-balanced and capable of standing off. When I visited this country I was riding an experienced local horse, and I was most grateful to be so mounted.

There is still plenty of grass in the Berkeley country, but moving into Berkshire and Buckinghamshire we see the dramatic effects of the postwar increase in plough. Yet the hunting here is as ardently supported as ever. The Bicester and Warden Hill's Thursday country, lying between Aylesbury and Bicester, and the Whaddon Chase's country, around Whitchurch and Mursley, still has plenty of grass, and there are some really big fences to be jumped.

These are lush, wet farming areas, and a hunter must be really fit to carry a heavyweight man across the deep going and over the uncompromising thorn hedges often guarded by broad ditches.

Dorian Williams has been Joint Master of the Whaddon Chase since 1954, and is a brilliant Field Master across this big country. He has always produced just the right sort of quality hunter of substance for these conditions, and likes them to have had some showjumping experience.

The timber can be big in these parts, as well as the hedges, and a horse must not turn its head at wire laced into an obstacle.

The Shires and Central Midlands

Traditionally the Shires are the 'capital' of foxhunting in England; other countries are known as 'provincial'. Nimrod, the great 19th-century hunting correspondent, frequently let it be known that Leicestershire was hunting's paradise, and all else was second best or worse.

Inevitably, there is a counter-reaction in the hunting field, and many a devout foxhunter 'wouldn't give you tuppence' for a day or a season in the Shires.

My own view is that you will find it difficult to have more fun anywhere else, for Leicestershire is still a superb setting in which to ride after hounds, but of course there is enormous fun to be gained wherever hounds hunt and it is profitless to argue the merits of one country against another.

The sighs for yesteryear are not infrequent in Leicestershire, for 'progress' has hardly helped foxhunting. The M1 motorway carved an uncompromising line up through the heart of the Midlands and other roads have become busier and wider.

Yet in the famous Quorn, Cottesmore and Belvoir countries the biggest change has been the loss of grassland since the 1930s, when all was a sea of green. The war saw much land ploughed up, and the trend to arable farming increased since then.

The most fashionable and popular days remain Quorn Mondays and Fridays, Cottesmore Tuesdays and alternate Belvoir Saturdays. These are the days when the areas with most grass are still hunted, and inevitably the largest fields of mounted followers are out.

I have had tremendous fun hunting on these days when hounds draw some of the most famous coverts in the foxhunting world. To gallop on the flank of hounds as they fly across the broad Leicestershire acres is a tremendous thrill.

The hunts perform a wonderful job in ensuring that there is very little wire in the best areas, and there are still plenty of superb fences to jump. Some who have only visited the Quorn's best Monday country are inclined to dismiss Leicestershire fences as 'not very big'.

In fact, the beauty of these countries is their immense variety. The traditional Leicestershire fly fence is a fairly simple jump for most horses, although modern farming tends to gouge a ditch or a scoop more efficiently, and alarmingly, alongside even the neatest hedge. But there are also plenty of very large fences, both timber and hedges.

But in Leicestershire your horse will usually jump far more fences in a run than in most other countries, and the tradition here is to keep the tempo up all day. The huntsman tends to canter on to the next covert to draw, and when the hounds go away, it is vital to get away well when the Field Master gives the signal or you may never make up lost ground in a 'quick thing' across the grass.

For all these reasons, it is essential to have two horses a day if you are to hunt regularly here. One good horse will doubtless manage a day, or most of it, especially if you are a lightweight, but the constant galloping and jumping, and the distances covered, impose a severe strain on a hunter, especially if you get into arable areas, for the plough here is particularly sticky and holding.

These hunts still list a site for 'second horses' during a day's hunting, and here the horse-boxes gather and grooms stand by with fresh horses, saddled up and ready to go,

as the mounted field arrives to hand over first horses. Of course, this has to be a fairly elastic arrangement as the vagaries of the chase may provide such a long, fast run in the morning that the riders do not get their second horses until late, or fail to collect them at all.

This is where the system of second horsemen can be invaluable. In the 'good old days' a back-up army of second horsemen followed the earlier part of the day's sport, carefully conserving their horses, but endeavouring to be on hand with fresh horses when most required.

The second horsemen wore livery and obeyed the instructions of the Master's own second horseman as to where they went and how they behaved. Many a top huntsman gained his early experience of the hunting field as a second horseman, and an excellent method it was of providing early experience before the young man could aspire to whipping-in.

The availability of modern motorized horse transport, and the cost of labour, makes the second horseman more of a rarity nowadays. But second horses are by no means confined to Leicestershire, although in many other hunts it is mainly the Masters and hunt staffs who have this facility.

I am a great believer in the system, for I am sure that more horses injure themselves when they are tired at the end of the day, and their working life in the hunting field is likely to be greatly extended and enhanced if they can hunt half-days.

Yet it is essential that stable management is alive to the problems of the second horse system. If sport has been particularly dull, or the weather has stopped hunting lately, it is all the more essential that hunters have their corn rations reduced accordingly.

Riding two 'fizzed up' horses which never get time to settle and work properly in their half-days is not much fun, and is not good for the horses. But two or three half-days a week is much better for a horse, properly conditioned and fed, than one long gruelling day in which it is all too easy to 'get to the bottom' of your mount's endurance. And from the rider's point of view, there is no better tonic after a tiring run than to mount a fresh horse.

Let me hasten to add that second horses are by no means essential to good hunting, but shorter days are inevitable if hunt staff cannot have two horses, and a follower should be considerate in taking home a horse that has had enough by 3 p.m.

The main difference which the newcomer finds in riding in the Shires for the first time is the enormous crowds of mounted followers on the more popular days. This is also true of the Duke of Beaufort's, the Heythrop and some other packs.

Some people never become accustomed to this, and gratefully return to the much smaller fields of their local pack at home. Yet there is nothing new about large mounted fields in the Shires. The enormous enclosures have always accommodated big crowds, although the needs of modern farming make it necessary for these hunts to restrict the numbers of visitors far more tightly nowadays.

There is a particular art in riding in these countries. The instructions of the Field Master are vital, particularly at the early stages, but much depends on the good sense and skill of each individual out hunting. You *must* keep a wary eye for planted fields which are not to be ridden over; you must *not* gallop among farm stock; and you *must* shut farm gates unless other riders are following.

There is still far less need to queue in these open, galloping countries, when it comes to jumping fences. In many provincial countries nearly every fence is a case of follow my leader.

If you are to keep anywhere near the 'top of the hunt' in a decent run in the Shires, you must be capable of pulling your horse out to jump without a lead; you must *not* be flurried or distressed by others jumping alongside you; you must not follow blindly right on the heels of the horse in front, for if he stops you will collide and, at worst, if he falls you may land on horse or rider.

Over-riding is one of the worst sins in the hunting field, and is far too often seen. It is no good being sorry afterwards, for this is one of the easiest methods of maiming or even killing the rider in front.

Similarly, if your horse has a tendency to kick out in crowds, then cure him of it *before* you sally to the Shires, or leave him at home. I have seen other people's knees smashed this way, or valuable horses permanently lamed because some idiot insisted on hunting a kicker.

The best remedy for a kicking horse is to thrash it soundly *immediately* it kicks. If more young horses were disciplined effectively in this way they would escape chastisement later in life, and they would be safer animals to take hunting.

Everyone knows that kicking a hound is a crime, but it is amazing how few people bother to turn their horses' heads towards hounds when they come close. There are many minor pieces of 'cross country craft' in the hunting field which, when added up, make the difference between a reasonably safe progress across country and an exercise which may be lethal for you and for others.

For example, some patches of road are much more slippery than others, and you should watch out for them in cantering along roads. Verges by roads often have narrow, hidden drains which can bring horses down so easily. A swinging gate you fail to catch may damage you, or smash into the person just behind. Jumping blindly onto a road may lead to a collision with a vehicle. Failing to pull up properly at a gateway can cause your horse to collide with the horse in front, possibly giving this horse a severe wound on the hind fetlocks or pasterns, or provoking it to kick your mount.

When someone has dismounted to open a gate, or take down wire, and you have ridden through the gap, it is not just sheer bad manners to gallop on and leave that person still on his feet. The swift departure of your horse may cause his to plunge and fidget, thus making it difficult or impossible for your benefactor to remount.

Refusing at a fence means that you should wait and go behind those just about to jump after you. Holding up other people by repeated refusals is one way of helping to ruin everyone's fun. Whether you realize it or not, sitting on a horse automatically puts anyone into a position where thoughtlessness looks like arrogance. So always be considerate with people on foot or in motor vehicles. You are towering above them, and we probably all have folk memories of being ridden down by advancing horsemen in the dim mists of history. I am sure this is one of the emotional strands in the motives of the anti-hunting protestors.

A cheery thank-you or good morning is so easy to dispense to those you meet in the countryside. Your behaviour will be one more factor influencing other people's judgement of hunting.

Northampton, the West Midlands and Wales

The Grafton and Pytchley countries in Northamptonshire and the Fernie, which was in the former county of Rutland, enjoy fame equal with the Leicestershire packs in the history of hunting. The change-over to plough was particularly widespread in the first two, although the Fernie—now in south Leicestershire—still has plenty of grass and is a very well run country, providing two days a week.

It was always said that the Grafton was the biggest country to ride in England. Having hunted there in recent years I would assert that it can still be very challenging, but alas the plough and wire have made it far more difficult than in its palmy days before World War II.

Great bullfinches, through which a bold horse must bore, huge ditches, and upright hedges with fierce growth in them are among the challenges here. The timber is seldom neat and small, and the Grafton has resisted the solution of saturating the country with hunt jumps. Much of it still has to be jumped 'in the raw', and if you wish to see how this should be done, watch senior Joint Master Col. Neil Foster, one of the best lightweights across country in the modern hunting field.

The Pytchley, similarly, has always been a tough, challenging country, and has seen a considerable change-over to plough, but it is still a most entertaining country to ride, and you need a good horse to follow hounds when they are running fast.

Shropshire and Herefordshire still have a lot of grass, although wire is a problem in many areas. The same applies to Wales where the terrain varies from easy to rough, yet the wild beauty of the hills and valleys, the hospitality of the hunting fraternity, and the 'self-hunting' propensities of the shaggy-coated Welsh hounds who will cheerfully hunt all night without the aid of a huntsman, make a visit to the Principality an unforgettable experience for the foxhunter.

One of the most attractive countries is undoubtedly Sir Watkin Williams-Wynn's which lies on the borders of Denbigh, Flint, Cheshire and Shropshire. There is plenty of grass and there are many jumpable thorn hedges, often guarded by wide ditches.

I much enjoyed this country, and I would describe it as one of the very best two-day-a-week countries in Britain. Just to the north, the Cheshire still abounds in grass, and the fences come faster than Leicestershire, since the enclosures tend to be smaller. Their huntsman, Johnny O'Shea, is one of the best natural riders across country to be seen, and he can certainly fly when hounds run hard.

In the West Midlands, Derbyshire offers some superb hunting country. Those black stone walls on the Derbyshire hills take some jumping, and I had great fun there in the South Notts Hunt's wall country round Belper.

The Meynell has superb grass vale conditions as well as a walled hill country, and its variety throughout the season must make it among the best hunting areas in England.

The North and Scotland

Yorkshire, Northumberland and Durham are all great foxhunting areas. They all benefit from the lack of urban sprawl compared with the South and South-east. You may hunt in the North sometimes with factory chimneys on the horizon, but there is no vast suburban area between you and the industrial town.

In Yorkshire I have had particularly good fun with the Zetland and Bedale. Both areas have great variety, with every sort of fence, and good open conditions where a hunt can be easily seen. Arable farming has increased enormously, but there is still plenty of grass.

Below
Jumping black stone walls is a speciality in Derbyshire. The Secretary of the South Notts Hunt shows how it should be done.

It is my impression that thorn does not grow so readily in the North, but fly fences are often well strengthened with timber.

The Middleton and Middleton East has a lovely upland wolds area as well as a vale. Here is a great tradition of foxhunting which the senior Joint Master, Lord Halifax, has maintained at a high standard.

In Durham and Northumberland I have especially enjoyed hunting with the Braes of Derwent and the Tynedale. The former is a lovely, wild country with walls which can take some jumping, and your horse needs to be able to manage rough going as well as some excellent permanent grass.

The Tynedale has one of the few true grass countries still in existence—a sea of grass in all directions, intersected with jumpable walls. It is hilly, and the amount of stock wintered out tends to be a problem from a hunting point of view. There has also been an increase in the amount of barbed wire guarding the walls, owing to the new anti-brucellosis regulations. Yet with the Tynedale a fast, blood horse is still a boon.

For a more open, marvellous sweep of grass or moorland you must go further north to the Duke of Northumberland's pack, the Percy, and its neighbouring hunts. I thoroughly enjoyed a day with the Milvain Percy. There was a run on good, galloping heather where I could observe the fox ahead, and then the hounds, and the huntsman was just in front of me. I could actually see the fox go to ground just in front of the hounds. Containing quite a lot of Fell blood, these hounds did not await the arrival of terriers, but swiftly dug out the fox themselves!

There are timber jumping places in the wire fences, and occasional walls, but it is for the gallop and the joy of following hounds in such beautiful, natural country, that a visit to the north is well worthwhile. You will also meet some of the truest sportsmen to be found anywhere.

I have never hunted in Scotland, but there is a great deal of pasture, with some plough, moorland and woodland in the famous lowland countries, such as the Duke of Buccleuch's. Again they suffer far less from urbanization than so many southern English areas.

Altogether, hunting in the north is warmly to be recommended, and the sport will continue here in its most natural form as long as anywhere. Yet there are two drawbacks I have not so far mentioned: the greater likelihood of severe winter weather causing the loss of hunting days through frost or deep snow; and the comparative scarcity of foxes in some areas, compared with the South. This is partly due to an apparent reluctance of the species to breed in such numbers in the North, and also to the proliferation of shooting interests in some Northern areas where the fox is killed not by foxhounds, but by gamekeepers.

Ireland

For variety, thrills, and all sorts of enjoyment, Ireland is to be strongly recommended to the foxhunter. I have never failed to have a marvellous time on hunting visits, and I am constantly captivated by fabulous views, and warmed by the hospitality of the natives.

Around Dublin is some of the most popular hunting country but I also recommend going further south and west if you can spare the time. Co. Meath, just outside Dublin, has some of the biggest ditches to be jumped by horses anywhere in the world. I encountered them with the Meath foxhounds, and with the Ward Union Staghounds who hunted carted deer twice week.

The deer is released from a horse vehicle and given eight minutes' start before hounds are laid on the line and usually proceed to race across country on the deer's scent. At the end of the run the deer is either allowed to wander free, or is boxed up again, and taken back to the paddocks near the hunt kennels where a number of red deer are kept for the purpose. Hounds never touch them during a hunt, and each deer only 'goes hunting' a maximum of twice a year.

The only other carted deer pack still in existence is the County Down Staghounds in Northern Ireland. At one time there were many of these packs in England, and they certainly do provide an exciting run across country as the deer has such enormous stamina and jumping ability, and usually leaves a strong scent.

The Co. Meath ditches yawn at you like ravines, among the most intimidating sights I have peered at between a horse's ears in the hunting field. The technique is to jump such a ditch from a standstill, but sometimes they are so wide that a horse will slide down the take-off side, and launch across to scramble up the opposite bank. They can be so deep that a horse and rider can disappear from view in the depths. I recall jumping a ditch while a horse and rider, still together, wandered along the bottom of the ditch below, seeking a way out after falling in.

Banks and walls are more frequent cross-country obstacles in Ireland, and they range from the very small to the almost impossibly large.

There are few clean banks nowadays, as there has been a tremendous increase in the thorny growth on them, and this makes them even more difficult to cross.

Some of the best of my fun has been with the Co. Limerick Hunt which has one of the biggest bank countries, and a separate area of stone walls, with grass everywhere.

In the Friday country your horse must leap a ditch, often of daunting width and depth, to land on the slope of the bank which may be more than 15-20ft (5-6m) high. Sometimes this seems to offer no foothold at all, and the Irish hunter—a magician on four legs—somehow clings to the near vertical surface. Then he crashes upwards through seemingly impenetrable thorn. He pokes his head through the far side, hovers for a second, and launches into space down over another chasm to land safely, even in hock-deep mud.

Once in the Tipperary country I followed the huntsman on to such a bank, then instead of jumping off on the far side, he turned his horse sideways and teetered along the top to a corner of the field where he met another bank. He then launched himself through a black hedge which closed behind him. I was left high on the bank, above what looked like a cross between the Grand Canyon and Cheddar Gorge.

It was unjumpable, and if we had fallen into it my fate could only have been discussed in hushed whispers. Fortunately, my hunter took matters firmly into his control, turning sideways and doing a similar 'high wire' act on the narrow top of the bank until he, too, hurtled off through the black bush. I opened my eyes to a curious sensation of flying, surely the nearest thing to being on a winged horse. Then we touched down with an enormous splash in a waterlogged field.

My hunter, all of five years old, somehow kept his feet and set off at a steady canter as if nothing had happened.

Opposite
Hunting in the snow: veteran former huntsman of the Warrenton Hunt Dick Bywaters in Hart's Mountain country in Virginia

Truly, Irish horses are marvels. They are said to learn their extraordinary skills through following their dams when grazing across banks as foals. This may be true in some cases, but it must be an inherited ability, and it is the Irish horse's curious ability to find a 'fifth leg' in emergencies which makes him one of the world's greatest cross country exponents.

Banks vary enormously, and there is a smaller razor-backed sort which requires a nippier skill, the horse skimming the top and changing legs neatly to ensure landing safely on a leading foreleg. Other banks are stone-faced, and require considerable boldness to ascend.

Irish walls vary from neat jumpable obstacles to enormous, craggy edifices which cannot be jumped, but must be climbed and banked. In the Kilkenny country I was constantly amazed that horses did not cut their legs to bits on such walls, but there were very few signs of cuts or grazes on hunters out that day. We crossed one stretch of country known locally as 'Murder Mile', with a stone wall every 50 yards or so.

The most famous wall country is, of course, in Co. Galway, home of the Blazers pack. This is all permanent grass, with neat, jumpable walls bordering small fields. You may jump 100 of these walls in no time at all. They are built of single stone thickness with gaps which the winds blow through. Such fields seldom have gates, as the sheep farmer simply takes down a few stones to get his sheep in or out, and then builds the wall up again.

A fox in the open here must run hard, and it is a tremendous thrill to gallop on the springy grass and take the walls as they come. Take-offs and landings may be of disconcertingly different heights, and nothing can be taken for granted.

At the edge of a field bordered by a lane, there was the inevitable wall. 'Nothing to worry about here,' said a friend who had already arrived in the lane through a gap further down.

I collected my horse and popped over the wall, only to find a drop of more than 15 feet onto tarmac. The Irish hunter managed it with aplomb, but my remarks to my friends could not be published!

Ireland is a great magnet to the hunting visitor because it is still possible to hire horses which will cross the country. Costs have increased tremendously in recent years, but it is well worthwhile to make the journey and put your hand deep into your pocket for a day or two in an Irish country.

There is hunting with harrier packs even on Sunday afternoons. Nothing else is quite like it, and each man must discover his own Ireland.

There are many gaps in my survey, but I hope to have shown that there is still immense variety, and a great, natural challenge to be met in riding across country in Britain and Ireland. I have written little about hounds or the science of hunting, since we are here concerned with the ride, but remember that when old age makes the falls more painful and the fences much less beguiling, it is the cry of the hounds which remains the imperishable attraction in the hunting field.

As Jorrocks once said, happy is he who goes hunting to amuse himself—and not to astonish others.

Opposite
Detail from 'The Grosvenor Hunt' by George Stubbs, the celebrated eighteenth-century English animal painter

Riding to Hounds in the United States

Jane McIlvaine McClary

The United States is the greatest foxhunting country in the world today as far as diversity of terrain and a unique variety of methods are concerned. Foxhunting, North American-style, runs the gamut, from the dressed-to-kill, artificial drags abounding in the suburbs, to the overalled zealots on a high hill listening to their 'dawgs' run a fox by moonlight in a distant valley.

In America the early settlers hunted to live. Today there are those who live to hunt—some by riding expensive horse-flesh over grass fields and high fences. These are the 'High Church' foxhunters who in the words of Evelyn Waugh 'tend to regard all forms of athletics as inferior forms of foxhunting'. They make the picture the world sees, the scarlet coats and fine horses, the great leaps and beautiful backgrounds. During the past decade Jacqueline Kennedy Onassis brought foxhunting alive for the American public in the same manner that H.R.H. Princess Anne popularized Combined Training in Britain. Like many famous people before her, the former First Lady of the United States provoked indignant remarks by neglecting ceremonial functions in favour of the chase. She once commented that in the hunting field she could lose herself and 'feel clean and anonymous'.

Until Jackie Kennedy made headlines by diving over one of Paul Mellon's split-rail fences on the art collector's Virginia farm in 1962, the great unbooted public considered foxhunting, if they considered it at all, something you did with a gun. The reaction of many was like that of the butler who, at first sight of hounds in full cry, leaned out of the pantry window and shot the hunted fox in full view of its pursuers. When converged upon by irate foxhunters he explained he thought he was doing them a service. His employer was all set to sack him when the lady of the house intervened. A non-foxhunter, she threatened to leave her husband if he gave the butler notice. Butlers, she argued, were a vanishing species, harder to come by than foxes or husbands.

Although England and Ireland still boast more foxes than you can shake a hunting whip at, the red fox, due to attrition by highways and housing developments, is growing scarce. The grey fox the early settlers hunted, indigenous to the south, climbs trees and prefers to run in circles. The red fox—a Mr Smith supposedly imported the first red fox from England to the Eastern Shore of Maryland in 1829—provides better sport. Consequently numerous hunts import red foxes from non-foxhunting areas. They are then fed, nurtured and cared for, sometimes more carefully than humans. One underprivileged family I know subsisted on chickens provided for the foxes. For a long time the hunt wondered why no traces of bones or feathers were ever found by the foxes' den.

In the US there are some 140 hunts recognized by the Masters of Foxhounds Association. Although organized foxhunting is modelled along the lines of hunting in Britain, its parent country, methods, fences, terrain and attitudes vary.

Because of the population explosion and ever-encroaching civilization, foxhunting today takes place, to a large extent, in exurbia, outside the cities. Where wire has replaced the natural fences, chicken coops (sloping boards placed over the wire) have been built. Logs have been laid on the walls to eliminate the sharp 'cap' rocks that can cut open a horse's knee. Because of the necessity to queue up single-file at these narrow artificial 'panels', foxhunting American-style lacks the slam-bang, alacazam style associated with England and Ireland.

Virginia and Maryland foxhunts are perhaps the closest equivalent to the British original. Before World War II there were few made fences. The landed gentry rode fast thoroughbreds over century-old turf, rail fences and dry stone walls, artfully built by slaves during the ante-bellum plantation era.

Virginia is often called the Leicestershire of America. The Piedmont at the foot of the Blue Ridge mountains has what is probably the most beautiful natural country left in the United States. It is a legendary land of gently rolling farm fields, meandering streams and woods which in the fall become a tapestry of scarlets, browns and golds against the background of pale blue mountains.

Here in 1905 Harry Worcester Smith, grandfather of Tommy Smith who won the Grand National on Jay Trump in 1965, dared to prove that his American hounds were superior to the English. The first American to hunt his own Grafton (Massachusetts) foxhounds and fly-jump his American thoroughbreds over the Irish banks where, as master of the Westmeath, he spent two seasons, he issued a challenge to the late A. Henry Higginson, then Master of the Middlesex. A series of historic matches were held in the Piedmont Valley in which Mr Smith's Grafton hounds bested the British.

The Orange County Hunt, The Plains, Virginia, borders the Piedmont. It, too, has a wide-ranging, open country of gently rolling pasture and woods and a variety of fences, walls, coops, rails and snake. The red or orange coloured American hounds are well matched and very fast, requiring blood horses and hard riders. In the past this hunt, known as the 'Millionaires' Hunt', was said to be the most exclusive in America. E. H. Harriman, the railroad tycoon, brought his hounds and horses and guests from Orange County, New York, to Virginia in 1903, via private railroad car, complete with gold faucets and a grand piano. Visitors were and still are only permitted to hunt by invitation from a member. Exceptions were made for Mrs Jacqueline Kennedy Onassis who hunted regularly while she was First Lady, but a Prince of Wales is said to have lost the chance of hunting because he did not spend the night with his hostess, a requirement which has led to some rude remarks and caused the hunt to be called the 'Toothbrush' hunt.

The Maryland hunts are made up of point-to-point riders. Many have ridden or will

Previous page
Mrs Jacqueline Kennedy Onassis, out hunting with the Middleburg Hunt, clears a chicken coop

Opposite
The Piedmont Foxhounds in woodland. Typically, Virginia, one of America's most favoured foxhunting areas, is a big galloping country with plenty of pasture and post-and-rail fences

ride in the Maryland Hunt Cup, America's greatest steeplechase, over the tall unbreakable timber which, because of its height and stiffness, gives rise to the name 'America's Aintree'. Here again fast thoroughbreds, current or former 'chasers, are ridden to hounds.

The same is true of Mr. Stewart's Cheshire Foxhounds at Unionville, an all-grass country with straight-up-and-down post-and-rail fences, that requires a fast-galloping horse and one schooled over timber. Pennsylvania boasts many fine foxhunts but most agree that there are none better than this English pack. Mrs. John B. Hannum has long hunted her late stepfather's hounds. Descended from one of the country's foremost sporting families, she is generally acknowledged to be one of the best women M.F.H.s running her hunt and many-acred Brooklawn Farms with an iron hand in a string glove.

While some of the famous hunts of yesterday have lost their countries to expanding suburbs, new ones have come into being, adapting themselves to their surroundings. One is the Middleton Place Hunt in the sandy, piney, swampy plantation country of South Carolina where "Ware Gator' takes the place of 'Tally Ho!'

Since 1741 deer and alligators have roamed over the ten-thousand acres where Henry Middleton built his historic rice plantation fourteen miles northwest of

Charleston. Charles H. B. Duell, a direct descendant of the remarkable American family that included the President of the First Continental Congress, a signer of the Declaration of Independence and America's first Ambassador to Russia, has restored the pre-revolutionary gardens and original stable yards to their pre-war magnificence. Three years ago this setting became the scene of one of the country's newest and most unusual hunts. The drag is laid along narrow, rutted, logging roads deep in the pine woods and cypress swamps. The pack consists of a mixed bag of American-bred hounds ranging from a clutch of orange-coloured Orange County (Virginia) hounds, several black and white Penn-Marydel, an odd Blue Tick or two plus an occasional house dog joining in for the fun. And fun it is!

In March the season's end is celebrated by a gala hunt ball, hunt and breakfast at Middleton Plantation. While the riders, tourists and photographers sample the contents of stirrup cups served on silver trays, the behind-the-scenes story of the self-sustaining world of the Carolina low-country farm is told with animals, artifacts and crafts. A young girl, wearing a period costume, makes candles. Another weaves. A mule-drawn wagon provides rides for the children. A tame deer leaps back and forth over the stableyard fence. Peacocks flaunt their feathers. Sheep, goats, ducks, geese and rabbits wander about the peaceable profusion.

Before you can cry 'Gone Away', hounds find the line and are off. The field travels at racing speed, two by two, stemming around slippery corners, slaloming between trees. Mini-Aiken type fences, oxers made of pine poles with boughs sticking up between the rails, wired to trees on either side of the trail, rise at sudden intervals. Would-be jumpers find themselves carried out by non-jumpers seeking to circumvent the fences. Some vanish into the impenetrable wood or alligator-inhabited swamp, failing to surface again until the hunt breakfast. The horses are mostly unshod due to the sandy going. They consist of quarter horses, Morgans, cow ponies and a few thoroughbreds off the racetrack.

A charming and gracious example of the courtesy and hospitality for which the south is famous is that of 'visiting' between runs. As the hunt progresses the pairs riding together change partners in order to meet strangers and 'visit' with people they haven't met or 'visited' with before.

In the desert country of the American west the coyote is the quarry. The Arapahoe Hunt, Denver, Colorado, is the only recognized pack in North America that hunts coyotes with English foxhounds.

Hunting takes place on the late Lawrence C. Phipps, Jr.'s Highlands Ranch, on the outskirts of the city, thirteen miles south of Denver's famous Brown Palace Hotel. A mile above sea level the 20,000 acre cattle range, featuring its own buffalo herd, has as its centre a vast, towered and turreted castle-like structure with a baronial fireplace large enough to roast one of the highly bred Herefords that roam the range.

Before his death last year at 88, Mr Phipps was the oldest active M.F.H. to be honoured by the Masters of Foxhounds Association. Because his youth and foxhunting apprenticeship had been spent in England, he wanted a live hunt and one as much like those in the Shires as possible. In 1929 he established the Arapahoe which, in spite of no foxes and a desert country, has all the pomp and ceremony and appointments of the Quorn or the Cottesmore.

In the absence of foxes, the coyote, native to the American West, was the natural quarry. After a lifetime of study Mr Phipps found the coyote, large as a police dog and twice as fast, to be harder to hunt than the fox. Coyote scent is lighter and lasts but a short time. Coyotes do not go to ground: they find an area where scenting is poor, causing hounds to lose. Or else they outrun the pack, with the result that a kill is rare.

Nonetheless sport is of the highest order. Because of the quality of the country and the quarry, the abilities of hounds, horses and hunt staff have been perfected. Over the years they have adapted and introduced their own unique methods.

At the kennels there is a stabling for seventy-two horses. On non-hunting days they are exercised around a dirt track, a dozen or more at a time, 'driven' loose, as though cattle, by one mounted cowboy.

The horses evolved from 'Beauty', a $5 investment in hound food, to the high quality Phipps-bred hunters. Most are by thoroughbred sires with a tracing back to polo-pony mares, plus a smattering of cold or quarter-horse blood. This combines the speed necessary to gallop over open ranchland and the handiness to avoid gopher and badger holes and negotiate the steep, sheer-sided, canyon-like walls of the dry stream beds.

Mr Phipps' original hounds came from a country as wet as Colorado is dry. His foundation stock were descendants of North Warwickshire's Random '11 and Duke of Beaufort's Cardinal '13, mentioned in David Brock's book *To Hunt The Fox* as among the ten best stallion hounds of the first quarter of the century. Additional drafts of similar bloodlines were later obtained from Mr Stewart's Cheshire and the late A. Henry Higginson, the American Master of the Cattistock.

Today the Arapahoe Hounds are remarkably uniform, tri-coloured and one of the best hunting packs in America. Much credit is due George M. Beeman, huntsman for the past forty years. At 67 he is still riding as strongly and boldly as ever. 'Hounds, horses, staff,' he says with justifiable pride, 'all home-grown!' Beeman's son, Dr Marvin Beeman, and daughter, Bunny Beeman Morgan, are whippers-in and maintain almost perfect team work.

A letter to *Horse and Hound* of 6 March 1948 described the country as 'rolling, part open ranch land where the going is very fast and good, part thick with scrub oak, pines and deep water courses . . . not easy to ride . . .'

There are no coverts. Draws take place along open ranch land where post-and-rail panels have been built in the wire fences with an equal number of gates along the routes most often travelled by the coyotes.

While drawing through the dry, dusty terrain, Huntsman Beeman occasionally takes time out for what he calls a 'Sislap'. This consists of letting hounds refresh themselves and clear the dust from their noses and throats by plunging into whatever water is available, a pond or watering-trough. This, he believes, helps them to hunt better.

Hounds must be disciplined not to riot or chase newborn calves. On the other hand they must have the nose and initiative to pick up the coyotes' lighter scent and follow the line, made doubly difficult by the fact that coyotes generally hunt in pairs. They also prefer rough ground and the advantage of scrub oak cover. Thus hounds are trained to cull one from the other and get it headed for open country.

The whippers-in are stationed some distance away, at points flanking the hounds as they draw. Because of high visibility they are apt to view before hounds find the line. When a coyote is viewed, up goes a cap. The huntsman raises his by way of acknowledgement and brings hounds on the run.

There is no holloaing or cheering hounds on. Beeman communicates with his hounds by whistling softly, yet clearly. The operatic efforts indulged in by many a huntsman would, he says, send coyotes fleeing to the snow-capped sweep of the Rocky Mountains that serve as a spectacular backdrop to the desert valley.

Ben Hardaway is as well known in the South as Mr Phipps in the West. As Master and Huntsman of the Midland Foxhounds, Columbus, Georgia, Benjamin H. Hardaway III is becoming a foxhunting legend in his fifty-plus lifetime. Hardaway is a successful contractor who would rather hunt than eat Georgia grits or construct the bridges and dams for which his engineering firm is known throughout the South. 'I've had hounds since I was a boy,' he says. 'Nights I don't count sheep. I count bitches and dawgs and the best combinations.'

Hunting with Hardaway (rather than behind him, for he likes his field to be right up with the hounds and sharing his enthusiasm) is as close to hunting with Ronnie Wallace or Thady Ryan as you can come to in the U.S. Hardaway has hunted with both of these great M.F.H.s and has adapted some of their savvy and expertise to his totally dissimilar country, as far a cry from the Heythrop or the soft green enclosures of the Scarteen as his shrill rebel yell from the mellifluent English horn.

Midland is the rough, hilly, woodsy, red clay country of west Georgia and Alabama, a trappy country with chicken coop panels over wire. Here Hardaway hunts his unique home-bred 'fox dawgs', combining the methods of the old-time farmer foxhunters with the more organized aspects of riding thoroughbreds over fences.

His hounds have not been bred for beauty or conformity, rather for drive and teamwork. Over a period of some thirty years (his wife Sarah says she has long taken second place to bitches whelping in the bedroom or by the kitchen stove) he has evolved what he calls a 'biddable' pack that runs together under the proverbial pocket handkerchief, under practically any conditions, and responds to his slightest command. 'Pick up those poodles and bring 'em here!' The founding sires came from the West Waterford, Ireland, and Northumberland. The White Fell border hounds from the College Valley predominate. This relatively settled, civilized strain has been crossed with the old 'July' strain of wide-ranging, hard-hunting individualistic hounds, or in local jargon 'fox dawgs'. 'July' was one of the most famous stallion hounds in the south. Farmers came from miles around, Hardaway says, to breed to 'Ole July'. 'The poor ole dawg was bred so many times that he plum wore out! Got so when he heard another farm wagon or pick-up truck coming, he took to the hills!'

Hardaway's hunting pack is extraordinary. It includes the elegant, pure-bred, prize-winning Gainsborough from the Heythrop ('The only English hound I ever had worth feeding') and Ebony, coal black with four white pads ('A pointer got into the kennels').

But beauty is as beauty does and this is one helluva hunting pack. When Hardaway's 'fox dawgs done struck' (the line) the Master and his black sidekick Jefferson Goodwin, known as 'Tot', think nothing of jumping wire or snow fences. They generate a sense of urgency and excitement and the cry of hounds, like Hardaway's high-pitched

Above
Author Jane McIlvaine McClary discussing the composition of the Midland Foxhounds with Benjamin H. Hardaway III, during the meet with the Warrenton Hunt in late October 1976

Below
Master and huntsman Benjamin H. Hardaway III with the Midland Foxhounds, following a meet at Grove, in the heart of the Warrenton hunting country

Previous page
Huntsman George M. Beeman
and the Arapahoe English
Foxhounds hunting coyote on
Lawrence C. Phipps, Jr.'s
Highlands Ranch near Denver,
Colorado

Confederate screech, is guaranteed to raise the bumps on a goose.

Countries and quarries, cap fees and subscriptions may differ radically, but the feeling, the passion for foxhunting, is the same. Behind every Brahman of the chase are legions of followers who deny themselves the necessities of life in order to keep a couple of 'fox dawgs'. No article on American foxhunting would be complete without mention of this individualistic and free-wheeling fraternity, who since the earliest days of the Colonies have kept a couple or more hounds.

To these foxhunters, called 'hill-toppers' or 'night foxhunters', the chase means a fire on a hill-top and an earthenware jug of moonshine (home-brewed corn 'likker') to be passed around during the night as they listen to their individual hounds' voices, running a fox in the distance.

Bets are placed as to which farmer's 'fox dawg' will win, lead the pack for the longest period, be first at the kill or when the fox goes to ground. Speed and gameness are required to avoid merciless taunts should a hound give up the chase before marking its quarry.

These night foxhunters know their hound pedigrees from the couple Noah transported on the ark to George Washington's French hound Vulcan which, following the time-honoured custom of giving hounds as courtesy gifts, was sent to the First President by Lafayette. These men will travel long distances to breed their bitches to well-known dog hounds. Occasionally their hounds take precedence over wives.

Mason Houghland, the eminent Tennessee M.F.H., tells of a young night hunter who had been courting the same girl for ten years. When asked why he didn't marry her he replied, 'I'm too poor to keep four hounds and a wife. She will marry me if I give up two hounds. But I ain't never been able to decide which couple to give up!'

This type of foxhunting is as old as the Colonies themselves. In 1539 one of De Soto's retainers described the Spaniards' embarkation for the Americas: '. . . six hundred knights . . . and his priests . . . his horses, hounds and hogs.' (The Spaniards later admitted that the hounds were utilized to hunt Indians rather than foxes.)

Robert Brooke, the first known U.S. Master of Foxhounds, was born in London in 1602, the son of Thomas Brooke, a Member of Parliament. In 1650 Robert sailed to America in his own ship, taking with him his family, a large retinue of servants (forty in all!) and his pack of hounds. Due to this importation Brooke hounds provided the tap-root of several strains that came to be known as American foxhounds—Trigg, Wade, and Walker, among others.

These hounds were bred for their ability to meet local hunting conditions. In certain parts of the country, notably the South where hound races still take place, the selection of the fittest during many generations developed a lean, fast hound that hunts at great speed under difficult local conditions of scent and terrain. These hounds carry little superfluous weight, yet, like the top quality thoroughbreds needed to keep up with them, they are able to stay for long periods, sometimes negotiating impossibly rough going, burned woods, plough, sandy wastes, brush, briars and rocky cliffs, dusty roads and frozen fields.

In Colonial times almost every farmer kept hounds which were permitted to run wild and forage for their food in order to keep them keen. The Colonists were avid foxhunters. There is scarcely a page in George Washington's diary that doesn't mention

toxhunting. Individual hunts, the runs, weather, scenting conditions and his companions of the chase were all carefully recorded. Each day the President's first thought was whether it was good for hunting. On hunting mornings breakfast—Indian corncake and a bowl of milk—was served by candlelight. ''Ere the cock had done salutation to the morn the cavalcade would have left the house.'

His wife Martha deplored the fact that even on days of important events he found time to indulge in his favourite pastime. Her housekeeping was also impeded by the hounds which lived in the house. Washington's favourite, Vulcan, is said to have made off with more than one joint that was being prepared for important guests at Mount Vernon.

Today the Rappahannock country is much as it was during Washington's time. The Indian name, meaning 'people of the ebb-and-flow stream', is derived from the river's fluctuating tides. Yet this Virginia county, founded on the headwaters of the river in the Blue Ridge mountains, remains relatively untouched by the tides of change. Here the mountain people live as they did in Colonial times, cultivating their crops and orchards by day, hunting foxes by night.

The annual Rappahannock point-to-point features an old-fashioned hound race. Excitement builds as close to a hundred hounds, home-bred and owned by individual farmers, are released from pick-up trucks. Although a drag is laid many vanish up a nearby mountain on the line of a live fox, failing to reappear for days.

Faint hearts never won a Rappahannock 'race' (the local term for a run). The Rappahannock foxhunter is a Tom Jonesian throwback to a time when a man was judged not by what he wore but by how he rode across a country. As most of the hunt members are occupied during the week—an old foxhunter once commented that the

Below
The old-fashioned hound race at the annual Rappahannock point-to-point

only two things that take all day are having a baby and foxhunting—hounds go out Sundays. Like Ireland's 'Sunday dogs' the field is made up of country people, some on hardy Irish-type half-breds that would look more at home between the shafts of a cart, some on foot and others in cars or pick-up trucks. Many wear jeans in place of breeches, rubber boots in place of Peel, cloth caps instead of velvet. Fortified by Rappahannock's special stirrup cup, home-brewed bourbon or bouillon mixed with sherry, you may find yourself leaving the meet at a full gallop, jumping a farm gate or going flat out over the point-to-point course.

When Rappahannock foxhunters call it a day they often wind up at Montpelier, the historic ante-bellum house (not to be confused with President Madison's Montpelier at Orange, Va.) where Washington spent many happy times foxhunting and socializing with his relatives in the County.

I remember one memorable party that took place in the clay-floored basement. 'Jim Bill' Fletcher, M.F.H. and local autocrat of the hunt-breakfast table, provided a black band that made music as wild as the snow-filled night. Fires blazed in all the basement fireplaces and a pig was roasting on a turning spit in the stone fireplace of the original kitchen where Washington rested his boots on the hearth after a long day with the hounds.

As the party and the night grew wilder a guest noticed several horses standing in the snow, looking cold and woebegone. Somebody suggested bringing them into the house. Room was made for them near the fireplace. There they stood for a long time, wet coats steaming from the heat, while a lady picked up behind them with a dustpan and brush. When the party ended the horses had fallen under the spell of Rappahannock's special brand of hospitality and refused to leave. In order to force them back out into the night it was necessary for their owners to beat them with brooms.

In Rappahannock today you see the same cider-coloured fields rising to meet the wooded foothills that Washington saw. Deer, foxes and an occasional black bear roam in the woods. Woodcock and wild turkeys fly. The weathered snake-rails and barways date from the original settlers who built them. The mountains are high, their ascents rough and steep, making it difficult to stay with hounds.

Some time ago, in an effort to avoid losing the pack, the Master and one of the whippers-in were equipped with walkie-talkies. At the meet the small boxes with shining new antenna rods were pocketed by the Master, 'Jim Bill' Fletcher, and whipper-in Jimmie Dodson, who was instructed to report on the pack's whereabouts. By the time the riders conquered the first mountain, the hounds were already out of sight, out of sound. As horses and riders stood catching their breath the Master unleashed his walkie-talkie and uncorked the shining new antenna.

'Do you hear me? Do you hear me? Jimmie, where are you? Where are the hounds? Over!'

There was a long silence, then sudden crackling. Everyone leaned forward eagerly. *'Hoy bebe Carta Blanca, la primera cerveza de Mexico!'*

The Master looked aghast. Instead of his whipper-in on the other side of the mountain he had somehow contacted Mexico.

Jim Bill tried again.

'Jimmie, Jimmie. Do you hear me? Speak to me. Over!'

Again crackling was heard. Then a sultry female voice.

'This is Pearl. How many fertilizer trucks can you spare?'

The male foxhunters, galvanized by the voice, clustered around.

'Find out who Pearl is,' one asked urgently.

'Pearl, Pearl . . .' the Master cried. 'Who . . . where are you? I'm on Fielding Mountain. Come in, please.'

'Hello,' the voice sounded exasperated. 'We want our drivers. Not *you* on Fielding Mountain. Joe's needed on a big job up the pike!'

The Master's face fell. 'Pearl, Pearl . . .' But Pearl had apparently had enough and could not be induced to 'come in, please'.

Everybody began talking at once. Suddenly a rider, who had stationed himself a distance away in order to listen for hounds, broke into the conversation.

'Who the h . . . is Pearl? I thought I heard Diamond!'

Jim Bill glared at his instrument and shook it. The crackling began again. Then came the long awaited voice of Jimmie, the whipper-in. 'This is Jimmie. The hounds . . . snap . . . crackle . . . pop . . .'

'Yes, Jimmie,' urged the Master. 'Go ahead, Jimmie. Jimmie, Jimmie, where in the h . . . are you?'

'I'm lost!'

At this point one vintage foxhunter yelled disgustedly, 'Shut that dam thing off! Diamond's found. Let's goooooo!'

A Stag Hunt in France
John Sedgwick

Hunting in France, in the sense that we understand it in this book, is known as *La Chasse à Courre*, to distinguish it from *La Chasse*, which, some would say, consists of shooting anything that moves, preferably before it starts to do so. There are about 120 recognized packs of hounds in France—the majority hunting in the forests of the centre and the west; from Picardy to Normandy and Brittany; and from the Loire valley to Poitou and into the Auvergne. In fact, except perhaps for Champagne and Alsace Lorraine, there are no provinces in France in which there is no hunting.

The main beast of venery is the stag, but the wild boar is still hunted in certain forests at some danger to man, horse and hound. The roebuck is hunted and so is the hare. The wolf is no longer available but rabbits are hunted in some parts! Regrettably, Renard the fox usually falls victim to the rifle.

The origins of *La Chasse à Courre* can be traced back for well over a thousand years to the Emperor Charlemagne by way of St Louis, who is reputed to have formulated the rules of venery, and the Bourbon royalty of France, but the French Revolution put paid to this noble sport for a time. It revived under Napoleon and has flourished since, despite such vicissitudes as three major wars (the first being that of 1870). Since the turn of the present century the sport has been carried on by the packs of the nobles and other landowners of France hunting in their own domains and to some extent in state forests. It is still conducted with great ceremony, much music and a general respect for tradition.

As a rule the hunts are now organized as societies or clubs of *Boutons*, members, under the mastership of the *Maître d'Équipage*, and the hounds are usually hunted by professional huntsmen, or *piqueux*, assisted by *valets de chiens*, or whippers-in and kennel men.

The hounds, properly *chiens d'ordre*, are descended from three or four main lines, but often with a large dash of the English foxhound; indeed as long ago as the 17th century Louis XIV imported English hounds for new blood. The lines are the *Français Tricolore*, a white hound with black and reddish markings, together with the *Blanc et Orange* ('White and Orange') hound; the *Blanc et Noir* ('White and Black'), a fairly heavy hound descended from the ancient *Bleu* ('Blue') of Gascony, and, finally, the *Poitevin*, a lighter tricolour hound. The foxhound tricolour cross seems to possess a good nose and a tenacious character, but unfortunately tends to hunt without giving tongue to any great extent.

In the nature of things, since hunting in France takes place in thick forests, there is more riding to hunt than hunting to ride; more so than is perhaps the case in England and Ireland where the terrain favours hard riding and leaping.

It was against this background that at 6 o'clock one black and wet, if mild, February morning, we left our house in Brittany to drive the short distance to our Anglo-French friends at the Manoir de la Houbarderie, en route for a meet of the Bourbansais staghounds in the Forêt du Gâvre, in the south of the province. There were lights on in the upper floor of the manor house as we approached; our friends were up and about, booted and spurred as it were. We drove on to the Château de la Bourbansais, a grand old 16th-century house at Pleugueneuc not far from Dinan, and the house of Comte and Comtesse de Lorgeril. Madame de Lorgeril is Vice-Master of the Bourbansais pack; the Comtesse de Gigou, of Langast, is Master.

Left
Staghunting in France in the Middle Ages

Opposite
The Russian André Grishin on Pavelets during the Junior European Horse Trial Championships at Pompadour in France in 1973

Above
A staghunt in progress in the
great forest of Fontainebleau.

Opposite
Sue Hatherly and Harley
competing at Badminton.
They were former winners at
Ledyard Farm and in the
Midland Bank Open
Championships in 1974, and
were members of the British
team at the European
Championships at Luhmühlen
in 1975

The hounds, *Anglo-Français Tricolores,* and the hunt horses had already left as we loaded our horses in the pitch black and drove off by Rennes, the capital of Brittany, south towards Nantes. The meet was advertised for around eleven o'clock, and there had been some suggestion that it was to be a joint meet with the Comte de St Germain's hounds, the Rallye Bretagne—but rumour is a lying *coquine.*

We had some hours' drive before us. For my part, I had seen something of the pack before, in particular at a meet the previous November at the beginning of the season in the Forêt de Loudéac, when the blessing of St Hubert was invoked by a parish priest standing in the pouring rain on the ramp of a horse-box. On that particular day they hunted their stag out of the forest and had to give him best, as hunting in France is confined to the forest and, since the Revolution anyhow, there is no right by custom to hunt at large. The priest obviously chose the wrong Saint, or the wrong day.

We drove on into the dawn and finally found ourselves in the small town of Guéméné-Penfao, just north of the du Gâvre forest. We stopped at the Café du Centre for refreshment and then drove on into the depths of the forest, arriving at the

A rare moment as the quarry
suddenly appears during a
staghunt near Fontainebleau

Left
Madame la Comtesse de
Gigou, Master of the
Bourbansais Hunt, en route for
a meet in the Forêt du Gâvre

crossroads *de la Belle Étoile* shortly before eleven o'clock. There was no one to be seen, and six roads and a number of rides radiated in all directions; but after some discussion we decided to try the road to La Piadière, which proved to be the right one. The doughty Daguet, the *piqueur*, who hails from Poitou, emerged on foot from a forest path with a favourite hound on a leash. He had been out since dawn and had a good report to make in his usual nonchalant way, as a result of which the Master, the Comtesse de Gigou, decided to change the venue to the southern end of the forest near the hamlet of La Turne, and the posse of vehicles now arriving wound its way into the forest to come out at a clearing. Soon the followers were in the saddle, with the hounds milling around Daguet who delivered his formal report to the Master with great aplomb, followed by a little horn-blowing by way of warming up.

The hunt uniform worn by the Boutons comprises a green coat with green velvet facings and gold lacing over an elaborate gilet, or waistcoat, white breeches and thigh-boots or top-boots. The Boutons carry a great circular horn worn round the body and a sword, the latter no mere decoration as we shall see later.

Some twelve couple of hounds loped off behind the *piqueur* who cheered them into the forest, his hound language obviously the Norman precursor of what is heard in England to-day. Without much delay they winded their stag and hunted up to him, bustling him up and down until they got him fairly away out of cover, over the clearing into the forest on the other side, from which he returned in due course running down-wind in the general direction of Le Gâvre village. The hounds hunted him well, losing him for a short time after half-an-hour, but then finding him and hunting him northwards, the *trompe* and *cornette*, horns great and small, sounding the ancient music of the chase. Eventually they ran into him by the main Guéméné-Penfao road where he took to the water and stood at bay. The pack forced him into deeper water and there was

a mêlée in the centre of the river as the hounds attacked. Eventually the stag regained the bank, to be despatched by one of the Boutons with a clean stroke of the sword to the heart, appropriate fanfares being played by another Bouton.

The hounds were then whipped off before they could break up their quarry and the stag's carcass was loaded into a van to be taken back to the meet for the final ceremony at the end of the day.

The *piqueur*, who had been close to his hounds throughout the chase, had had a bad fall, his horse rolling on him in a bog, but he was not seriously hurt and soon got going again—and at this point I must recount the gallant action, at the kill, of an English member of the field. Left to hold the horse of one of the Boutons and no doubt temporarily under the impression that there was a similarity of technique between *La Chasse à Courre* and the hunting of the otter, he plunged on his horse into the stream, the led-horse following, to cut off a possible line of retreat for the stag—only to find his horse's head disappearing under the muddy waters of a river deeper than he had anticipated. The led-horse easily regained the bank but the rider and his horse had a good bit of swimming to do. The intrepid mariner was found a little later standing under a tree emptying a large quantity of unpleasantly brown water from his saturated boots, a woebegone horse standing beside him. The habitual politeness of the French was maintained and condolences took the place of what in England would have been ribald remarks.

Below
After the fanfare at the end of the day, the hounds are at last rewarded

Now everyone, horse and foot, returned with the stag to the meet, where he was skinned and dismembered for distribution in the neighbourhood; trophies were presented with ceremony and finally the antlered head and various parts of the beast including the tripes and other entrails were neatly arranged on the ground for the final act. With the Boutons paraded in echelon behind the flesh, the hounds were brought on again and a veritable concert of hunting-music followed, including the fanfare *La Bourbansais*. After that the hounds were at last cheered on to their belated *petit déjeuner*.

But this was by no means the end of the day: an invitation to dine followed, and the Boutons and their guests made their way to an inn on the edge of the forest, first to refresh themselves with whisky and Perrier and then to sit down to a meal of the type for which France is famous, liberally accompanied by the wines of Burgundy.

At the end of the meal the river-going hunting-man, called on by Madame la Comtesse, the Master, made a speech in fluent and elaborate French in which he attributed his accident to the aptitude of Breton horses for fishing, the Bretons being a seafaring race if nothing else, and finished by asking the Master's permission to turn out in future in a bathing costume of green velvet and gold, with the hunt button. The author had the honour of proposing the toast '*à la Chasse à Courre*' which was drunk with acclamation, three times three, as they used to say.

During the meal, great interest was shown in foxhunting in England and Ireland and it appeared that several members of the hunt had ridden to hounds in those countries and enjoyed it. I hardly need to add that they themselves are very hospitable when they have Anglo-Saxon guests.

When we left the auberge to return home the moon was riding high in a stormy sky and by the time we were back at the Château de la Bourbansais with the horses it was half past two in the morning and pouring with rain again. The animals must have been glad to return to the warmth and comfort of their straw-littered stalls.

STEEPLECHASING

Steeplechasing first appeared in Ireland around 1752, owing its name to the practice of riding across country from one village church steeple to the next.

The National Hunt Committee in Britain (whose name reflects the intimate association between hunting and steeplechasing in their origins) was formed in 1866 to administer 'chasing under rules. The rules define permitted sizes of jumps, the numbers of obstacles of different types that are to be included in a course, and so on. The Committee was amalgamated with the Jockey Club, which controlled flat racing, in 1968.

Point-to-points are also run under the control of the Jockey Club, which requires that only horses that have been out hunting a certain number of times in the season, and amateur jockeys, should take part.

The Grand National, begun in 1837 and run at Aintree every year since 1839, was for long unrivalled at the centre of British steeplechasing, and Red Rum's hat-trick victory in 1977 has added a new dimension to the Aintree legend. Sandown, Kempton and in particular Cheltenham, where the spring National Hunt Meeting is held, are among the most popular National Hunt courses.

The Colonial Cup at Camden in South Carolina is the climax of the American season. The Maryland Hunt Cup is the most famous of the so-called timber races, a speciality of Maryland and Pennsylvania, where the jumps are solid timber fences up to 5ft (1.50m) high.

French steeplechasing is in many respects closer to its hunting origins than is the case in Britain and America, with more twisting courses and a wider variety of obstacles, and indeed some of its races are called Steeple-Chase-Cross-Country. Auteuil, where the Grand Steeplechase de Paris is run, is the premier French circuit, and there are as many as 150 provincial steeplechasing courses.

Bill Smith on Fort Devon at Kempton, January 1977

Steeplechasing in Britain
John Oaksey

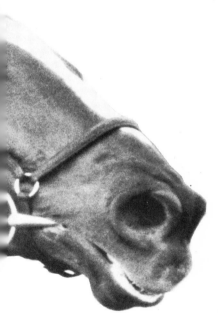

When, in the mid-18th century, two Irish hunting men called Blake and O'Callaghan challenged each other to ride across country 'from Buttevant Church to St Mary's Steeple' they probably had nothing more serious or far-reaching in mind than a test of their own horsemanship and their horses' agility and speed.

If, 225 years later, you could transport them by time-machine to a point half way down the Railway Straight during a two-mile steeplechase at Sandown—or even to the landing side of Becher's Brook in a Grand National—they would probably not recognize much connection between their carefree spur-of-the-moment jaunt and the carefully regulated chaos of a modern British steeplechase. But the line of descent is nevertheless direct, and the peculiar sporting urge which drove Messrs Blake and O'Callaghan across the fearsome banks of County Limerick is still alive and flourishing at Sandown Park, at Aintree and on forty-one other racecourses in Great Britain.

Ever since men rode horses they have no doubt argued over whose was fastest, and it was presumably just such an argument that inspired that first recorded 'steeplechase' in 1752. All horse-races are designed to answer the same fundamental question but in attempting to answer it 'across country'—and therefore over obstacles—the British discovered their own special brand of excitement, different from and, at least arguably, greater than anything obtainable from other forms of riding, and rivalling flat racing in popularity.

In some respects admittedly the thrills and hazards in those early days must have been very different from what a jumping jockey faces now. There was, for one thing, a far bigger element of uncertainty and choice—the right to choose your own line and the knowledge that both your neck and the result might depend on choosing correctly.

The word 'steeplechase' meant very much what it said—church steeples were the best and most outstanding landmarks, easily visible from a long way off even if you were in the middle of a blackthorn hedge or clambering out of a muddy ditch. The name underlines the difference between then and now and shows why local knowledge and an eye for country were in those days weapons every bit as vital in a rider's armoury as balance, stamina, or nerve.

In fact, when foxhunting men first wanted to test themselves and their hunters they

Above
An oil painting of
point-to-point steeplechasing
by the nineteenth-century
English artist H. Alken junior

did not even choose a course—but preferred to stage so-called 'pounding matches'. You tossed up or drew lots, it seems, and, if you won, had the doubtful privilege of setting off in front to take the stiffest line you dared as fast and far as you were able. Your objective was to 'pound' the other fellow until either exhaustion or the obstacles laid him low—his was to catch up and 'pound' you likewise in return. Not surprisingly this system ended, more often than not, in disaster and even by 18th-century standards some of the disasters were considered unacceptably horrific. But even when pounding matches were abandoned in favour of races from steeple to steeple it was still half the battle to choose the best and fastest line. 'I'll save you a hundred yards if you come through my garden', Lord Forester was told by a helpful admirer before his three-sided match with Charles Meynell and Sir Gilbert Heathcote. But over eight miles from Barkby Holt to Billesden Coplow a hundred yards was not, as it turned out, nearly enough. Meynell knew the country best and the knowledge got him home in front.

Even when steeplechases began to be run over more or less marked-out courses in the 19th century, the fences were often still left almost entirely 'natural', so their size and degree of difficulty were apt to vary sharply depending on where you chose to jump. In an early Grand National, so the story goes, one cunning competitor thought it worth his while to go round the night before, putting bits of ribbon on the best and easiest places. No doubt he went to bed happily confident of finding the perfect line next day but unfortunately his stratagem had been spotted by a rival—who crept out at the crack of dawn and moved the ribbons to all the biggest, hairiest locations!

Even nowadays, needless to say, it is still desirable to walk an unfamiliar course

Above
1976 Grand National runners jumping the 'chair', one of Aintree's most formidable fences. The eventual winner, Rag Trade (ridden by J. Burke), is jumping the fence second from right.

with care, and quite often the conditions produced by an English winter make it worth steering round the wide outside in search of elbow-room or faster ground. But although there is still plenty of scope for originality and initiative in a steeplechase, modern jumping jockeys do at least know (well, almost always) what to expect on the other side of the fence. At any given moment the course they choose to steer is still important but the basic thrill of taking your own line and proving it right the hard way is a thing of the past. With luck you can still just occasionally find it out hunting and certainly the nearest I ever came to guessing how Messrs Blake and O'Callaghan may have felt was in County Limerick, Ireland, with the Black and Tans, as the Scarteen fox-hounds are generally known. If, in that country, by some mischance, you find yourself forced to attack one of those barbed-wire- and blackthorn-encrusted banks *without a lead* you begin to know what 'taking your own line' really means. With Pat Hogan, Alan Lillingston or some such kindly expert to show you the way it is a comparatively easy matter—just a question of finding a good-enough horse, and hanging onto the neck-strap tight enough not to fall off or job him in the mouth. But if you are without a guide, the bank looks suddenly that much higher, the thicket on top of it that much harder to get through, and on the other side—who knows?

That was the sort of situation the original cross country riders faced as a matter of course. They were, in every sense, pioneers and we who have so simplified and bowdlerized their sport can only raise our crash helmets (of which they had never even heard) in respectful, admiring salute.

But if suddenly cross-examined now by one of those pathfinders we would still have a good deal to be proud of—and plenty of evidence to show that the pleasure and excitement of jumping steeplechase fences at speed is at least as widely understood and recognized in the 20th century as it was in the 18th or 19th.

We could describe to him a sport whose season lasts for ten months every year and which, for nearly five of those months, holds the centre of the racing stage without competition from the flat. Almost every weekday from November to March inclusive, weather permitting, at least two jumping meetings are held somewhere in the British Isles.

Admittedly more than half the races are run over hurdles and I don't suppose Messrs Blake and O'Callaghan would think much of an obstacle less than 4ft (1.20m) high. Come to that they might not think much of our steeplechase fences either—4ft 6in (1.30m) of tight-packed birch, but perhaps not, to their eyes, very dreadful compared with a Limerick double bank.

'But what about the speed?' we might reasonably ask and, from their magical vantage point halfway down the Railway Straight at Sandown, they would surely have to admit that the 18th century never saw anything to approach it.

It was $4\frac{1}{2}$ miles from Buttevant Church to St Mary's Steeple and history does not relate how long Messrs Blake and O'Callaghan took to get there. But their eyebrows, I hope and confidently expect, will rise in astounded admiration when we tell them that Red Rum and Crisp covered just that distance in 9 minutes 1.90 seconds in the 1973 Grand National. And even if the Aintree fences have nowadays been sloped and made a trifle easier they are still not exactly up-turned dandy-brushes. In fact, come to think of it, Richard Pitman, who rode Crisp that memorable day, must have in the back of his mind as good a picture as any man alive of how it feels to ride a big brave horse at speed over fences 5ft (1.50m) high.

His experience was shared, thanks to television, by an audience of many millions and in the matter of audiences too we may surprise our sporting forefathers. To watch one of their early steeplechases you needed a horse nearly as fast as those taking part—and the nerve to jump at least some of the obstacles. There were no grandstands to speak of and, if there had been, those who occupied them would have seen precious little of the action. Admittedly crowds built up tremendously between the two world wars, especially at Aintree. But even then the racing was seen and enjoyed by only a tiny fraction of the audience which now watches it on television every Saturday afternoon throughout the winter. Of course television keeps potential paying racegoers at home but it also demonstrably swells the betting turnover and, whether we like it or not, it is on the levy collected from that turnover that the fragile finances of British racing now depend. On the other hand, it has brought the thrill and spectacle of jumping into so many homes where hitherto they were unknown that it must, on balance, have done more good than harm, for undoubtedly some who have first enjoyed the sport on television have been encouraged to go and see it in the flesh.

Indeed, there can be no doubt at all about the part television has played in the post-World War II transformation of the jumping scene. Two central features of that transformation have been a decline in the importance of the Grand National and the advent of the sponsored race. They are closely connected, and television contributed to both.

Opposite
Rag Trade, winner of the 1976 Grand National, crashes at the final fence in the Kim Muir Memorial Challenge Cup in 1975

Until World War II the whole winter season was dominated by thoughts of and plans for the Grand National, originally founded in 1837, and acquiring its present name ten years later. It was the one really worthwhile steeplechase prize and any jumper who showed the slightest sign of having the necessary ability was immediately and exclusively aimed at Aintree, where the race has been run from the very beginning. Even the National Hunt Meeting at Cheltenham was in those pre-war days heavily overshadowed by the National and although Golden Miller won five Cheltenham Gold Cups in the 1930s it was his record-breaking victory at Aintree and his subsequent tribulations there that made him jumping's first genuine 'star' celebrity. At that time it would have been unthinkable for a steeplechaser to become anything like a household word (which Golden Miller certainly was) without running in the National.

However, Aintree has never been a good spectator's course. Even when visibility is excellent (not all that often when it matters most, in March) much of the action can only be seen in distant miniature and then only with first-rate binoculars from a vantage point on top of the Grandstand. And even those who have paid to achieve that fortunate position cannot hope to get more than a fraction of the close-up detail now provided at every single fence by BBC television.

Inevitably as the BBC developed and improved its coverage Aintree attendances began to dwindle and finally Mrs Topham, whose family firm had bought the course from Lord Sefton in 1949, declared her intention of selling it to a property development company. There followed a long and costly legal wrangle, and then year after year of publicity about the 'last' Grand National, none of which did Aintree or the great race any good. Eventually Mrs Topham did sell but Aintree's new owner, Mr Bill Davies, found the course no more of a gold-mine than she had. Again the end was threatened and it is only the intervention of the bookmakers Ladbrokes in 1976 which appears, for the moment at least, to have rescued and maybe even revived the home of the world's greatest steeplechase.

While all this was happening the whole emphasis of the British jumping season was moving away from the Grand National. The extent to which things have changed since the 1930s is illustrated by the fact that between 1961 and 1967 Arkle became at least as famous as Golden Miller throughout the sporting world—without once even being entered for a race at Aintree.

There are many—and I am among them—who believe that Arkle was in fact a greater horse than Golden Miller. We who hold that view are convinced that he could have won any Grand National, but his devoted owner, Anne, Duchess of Westminster, would never risk her beloved horse in the chancy free-for-all at Aintree. Arkle, however, was a far better, more accurate and more consistent jumper than Golden Miller and, barring sheer bad luck, I do not believe that the National fences would have caused him any more trouble than those over which he made his name at Cheltenham, Sandown, Newbury, Leopardstown and Fairyhouse.

Left
Mud flies as jumpers clear the water jump at Newton Abbot, May 1976

Arkle's career was made possible not only by the decline of the Grand National but also by the corresponding increase in the prestige of the Cheltenham Gold Cup and the appearance of valuable, commercially sponsored steeplechases like the Whitbread and Hennessy Gold Cups, brought into being by television whose coverage encouraged businessmen to use races as advertisements for their wares.

The Grand National, a handicap in which all horses are allotted weights which in theory give them an equal chance, has never been in any sense a 'championship'. Since the second war for every category of jumper—from seasoned three-mile 'chasers to four-year-old hurdlers—the real championships have been held at Cheltenham in March, although the three-day National Hunt meeting there, while undoubtedly the season's climax, has never had anything like the top-heavy over-balancing effect on the sport which the Grand National had before the war.

Instead, thanks largely to commercial sponsors, there is a steady flow of valuable prizes for both steeplechasers and hurdlers throughout the winter. For the sort of horse who in the old days would have trained exclusively for Aintree, the Hennessy Gold Cup provides a valuable target in November, the King George VI Chase is run at Kempton on Boxing Day, Cheltenham and the Gold Cup itself come in March and then whether you go to Aintree or not there is still the Whitbread Gold Cup at Sandown in April. For hurdlers the Schweppes Gold Trophy started a similar trend and in every age group hurdlers are now well catered for throughout the season.

One of jumping's biggest problems in fact is the huge number of refugees from the flat, who come into the sport as hurdlers each season—and the tiny proportion of them that ever trains on to make the grade as steeplechasers. Almost any flat-race horse can become a 'hurdler' of sorts. Granted the necessary ability and a certain minimum of physical and mental toughness, he may even earn all or part of his keep. But although such horses can and sometimes do learn to jump fences in time most of them lack the extra strength and substance which is needed to survive the rigours of a long steeplechasing career.

To all such generalizations there are glaring and glorious exceptions. The great Red Rum, for instance, has the pedigree of a sprinter and was bought as a yearling (by that great jumping jockey Tim Molony) specifically to win a five-furlong selling race on the flat. He won it too (dead-heating, believe it or not, at Liverpool on Grand National day) but he has since proved an exception to many old and hallowed rules, becoming the first horse since the 1930s to win three Nationals.

The fact remains that the vast majority of successful steeplechasers were in the first place bred for the job with at least some specialist jumping blood in their pedigree. And they were also given time to develop and mature far more gradually than Red Rum.

Unfortunately, however, fewer and fewer breeders can now afford the long, slow, and infinitely chancy business of producing and rearing such animals. The result, inevitably, is a glut of would-be hurdlers and a serious shortage of good experienced 'chasers'. Clerks of Courses who put on races for novice hurdlers are apt to find themselves compelled to split them into two, three or even four divisions. Their courses are ploughed up, numerous broken hurdles have to be expensively replaced and the end-product as far as the paying customer is concerned is apt to be an eight- or nine-race

Opposite
Hurdle racing at the Fair Hill races

Opposite
John Oaksey and Royal Relief
fall at the first fence in the
1974 Grand National at
Aintree

programme of two or three steeplechases with single-figure fields, and at least six overcrowded, more or less identical, hurdle races.

The danger of this imbalance in the long term is of course that hurdlers and hurdle racing may come to dominate the sport so much that steeplechasing begins to die out altogether, or to be watered down and emasculated to suit a lighter, more fragile type of horse. The nearer we get to that disastrous state of affairs the less the jumping jockey will have to know about real 'cross country riding'. But, as I hope to show, we are not near it yet.

Above
The legendary Red Rum, ridden by Tommy Stack, clearing the last fence in his history-making hat-trick victory in the Grand National in 1977

As I said to begin with, although the old and honourable art of taking your own line over obstacles is now largely a thing of the past, some remnants do survive.

At the start of a Grand National for instance you still have to choose your path over the six fences which culminate in Becher's Brook. The famous drop on the landing side there is noticeably deeper near the inside rail and many believe that by going a slightly longer route you give yourself a better chance both of surviving Becher's itself and of avoiding interference. On the other hand no less an expert than Fred Winter believes that the risk of the bigger drop is well worth taking—not only because it is a shorter route but because you are then better placed on the inside of the sharp left-handed swing over the fence after Becher's and the Canal Turn. Fred proved his point as a jockey on Sundew and Kilmore—and again as a trainer when his orders were followed to victory by Tommy Smith on Jay Trump and Tim Norman on Anglo. The evidence is pretty

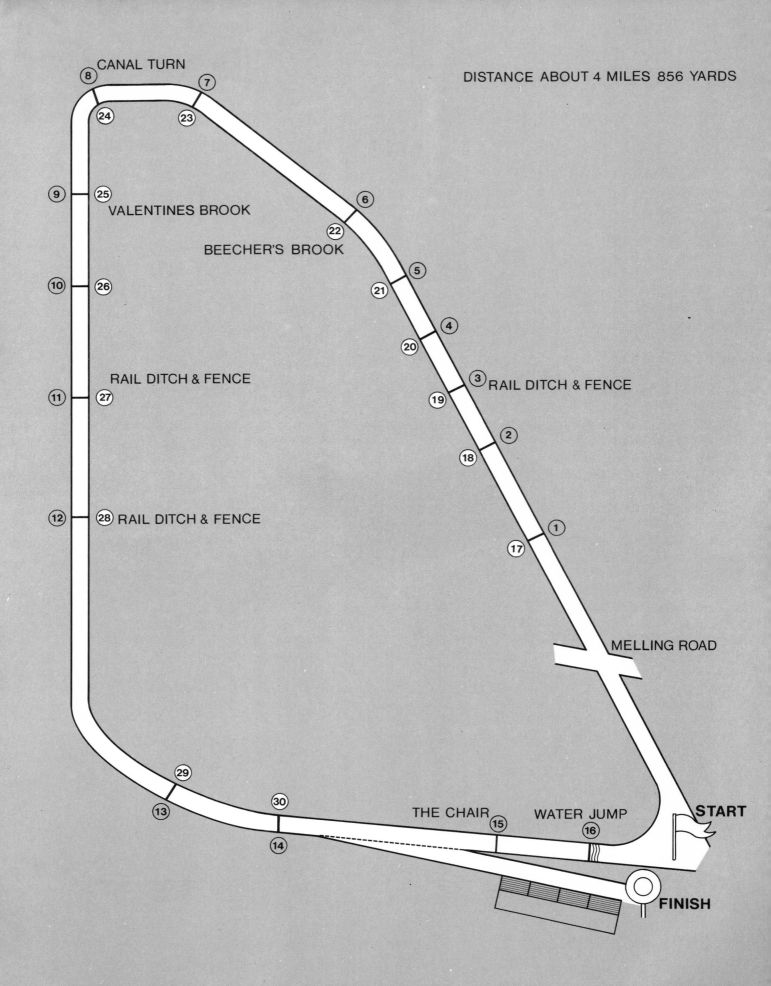

CANAL TURN

DISTANCE ABOUT 4 MILES 856 YARDS

VALENTINES BROOK

BEECHER'S BROOK

RAIL DITCH & FENCE

RAIL DITCH & FENCE

RAIL DITCH & FENCE

MELLING ROAD

THE CHAIR

WATER JUMP

START

FINISH

Opposite
The Grand National course at Aintree

Below
Uncle Bing with J. Francome at the water jump, Newbury, March 1976

formidable but habit dies hard and personally, having always gone down on the outside (on Pat Taffe's advice in the first place), I would always do so again if (which is unlikely) I ever got the chance.

In fact, in most recent Grand Nationals Becher's has seen no very serious pile-ups and even as we sailed over it in Foinavon's year, 1967, there were still more than a dozen of us left going well enough to have hope still alive in our hearts. It would be nice to claim that John Buckingham won on Foinavon because he 'chose the right line', but in fact as John freely admits his luck consisted of being so far behind that the chaos at the 23rd fence had begun to sort itself out by the time he arrived!

The extraordinary thing about that unique equine. traffic-jam was that Popham Down, the riderless horse who caused it all, had jumped Becher's perfectly, straight as a die. No one near him had any reason to fear that he might suddenly swerve and run down the 23rd—which is not only a very much smaller and easier fence than Becher's but has no frightening drop on the landing side.

Indeed, by knocking over three of the leaders Popham Down succeeded in making the fence quite literally unjumpable. I had been enjoying a marvellous ride on Northern but there was at least one horse lying in the bottom of the 23rd when we reached it and, taking off a full stride too soon in order to clear him, poor Northern landed smack in the fence itself. I went straight on without him—and arrived on the far side simultaneously with Stan Mellor. The thought uppermost in both our minds was how to get the hell out of there before the rest of the field came over on top of us—so the caption of a picture in next Monday's *Daily Telegraph* was a trifle flattering. 'Stan Mellor and Mr J. Lawrence [as the author was then] running in search of their horses,' it said—but 'running to save their skins' would have been a good deal more accurate.

But I digress. It is perfectly true that modern steeplechase courses no longer provide much variety and that fences in general are softer and less formidable than they were before World War II. But although this trend has undoubtedly altered the art of cross country riding as far as British jumping jockeys are concerned, it has not, in my perhaps prejudiced opinion, made their job any less difficult or exciting.

Steeplechases are, for one thing, run at a very much greater pace than before and the style and method of riding in them have had to develop and to be adapted accordingly. To begin with, when races were run across almost entirely natural country, men rode very much as though they were out hunting because the problems were much the same. Survival was far more important than wind resistance or speed, and the basic rule was that you could not win unless you stayed on the horse and kept him on his feet.

Needless to say, that rule still applies but anyone now who uses the old-fashioned hunting seat in a modern steeplechase would not only stand out like a sore thumb but would also, much more to the point, gravely impede his horse's progress.

The change started, perhaps, when Tod Sloan revolutionized flat-race jockeyship by introducing short stirrup leathers and the forward crouch from America. His immediate and undisputed success persuaded the flat-race fraternity, however reluctantly, to follow his example; but the jumping jockeys of the time were understandably much harder to convince. It was only very gradually that a typical British compromise was reached—a halfway house between the two extremes designed to achieve the balance and streamlining of the forward seat without sacrificing too much in terms of security.

When trouble comes, when a horse hits a fence halfway up at 25 mph or more, the natural tendency is for the jockey to go straight on. The horse may not fall but that's no consolation if you are lying on the ground watching him gallop away. That is where the stylish 'forward seat' would almost certainly send you—so it has to be adapted to cope with sudden violent deceleration. In the last split-second before take-off the expert will have seen disaster coming and moved to counteract it. His feet are thrust forward to absorb as much as possible of the shock and his fingers relax on the reins allowing them to slip so that he can avoid being pulled straight over the horse's head. Given freedom to stretch his neck the horse, despite landing too steep for comfort, may still with luck

Above
Moon Trip (jockey J.
Francome), right, disputes the
lead with Monfire (R.
Champion) at Windsor in
March 1976

'find a leg' and struggle on. The blunder will have cost him ground and energy but if
you the jockey are still there it may not cost the race.

Balance, grip, quick reactions and a correct technique all play their part in such
escapes and even they together may be useless without a fair share of luck. What looks
from the stands like an insignificant error may, if the horse screws sideways in mid-air or
lands crooked, send you willy nilly into orbit. The dreaded words 'unseated rider' go
down in the form book—and only the jockey knows how much or how little they were
deserved.

Even if the obstacles he has to jump are more or less uniform and predictable the
modern jockey must above all be able to adapt himself to different circumstances. In the
ten months of an English season he will have to ride through every variety of going and
weather from bright sunshine and rock-hard ground to driving sleet and a hock-deep
quagmire. The courses he rides on will range from the grandeur of Ascot to the bucolic
holiday atmosphere of Cartmel, from the big, green fences of Aintree to the little brown

birch ones of Taunton. Uphill and down, left-handed and right, they vary in countless different ways and, plying between them throughout the winter, a leading professional will cover the best part of 40,000 miles a year by road, much of it in the dark when he is tired, hungry and quite often bruised as well.

He will need to deal with big, hard-pulling Irish-bred geldings and light-framed, blue-blooded, temperamental colts. Even if he is lucky enough to ride mostly for trainers who school their charges patiently and well, a jockey will have to ride many indifferent, inexperienced or downright dangerous jumpers. And even on the good, experienced ones he must always be ready to cope with an unexpected, unforeseeable mistake.

One of the many things which in my opinion makes one ride in a steeplechase worth a dozen or more on the flat is that even *bad* rides can give you pleasure and satisfaction.

Above
Village Slave (J. Burke) leads the eventual winner, Floating Pound (J. Francome), over the final open ditch in the Embassy Premier Chase at Chepstow, November 1975

Of course they may also give you crashing falls but in a young horse's first few steeplechases every single fence presents problems which you may or may not be able to help him solve. Suppose, for instance, that he is a hard puller apt to run away or tear into his fences too fast to jump if shown much daylight. How long can you afford to keep him 'covered up' behind another horse? Will the jockey you are tracking pull out in time to let you see the fence? Does your horse need a kick to take off or would he jump better if you leave him alone? All these and many other questions will be answered one way or another by the finish and even if you get there far behind the winner you may still have a real sense of achievement.

But, of course, the satisfaction of helping to teach a horse his job is nothing compared with the thrill you get when he has learnt it. For all the black parts of a jockey's life, the falls, the wasting and the broken bones, the blame when you get beat, the long drive home, the bitterness of having someone 'jock you off'—all these are easily and quickly swept away in just a few exhilarating minutes when the dice roll right. Then, on a good experienced jumper whom you know and trust, a steeplechase is pure joy from the moment you get a leg up in the paddock until you ride back, hot, tired and blissfully happy, into the winner's enclosure.

In the minutes between you have probably not done anything very difficult or clever because riding good experienced jumpers over fences is mainly a matter of 'going with them' and interfering as little as you can. Some 'chasers, even seasoned ones, may like and expect an encouraging squeeze for the last two or three strides before taking off—but anything more than that is a dangerous and unnecessary example of 'teaching your grandmother to suck eggs'. Quite often old horses simply ignore any 'command' of which they don't approve and a superlative jumper I used to ride called Tuscan Prince invariably made up his own mind as to where to take off quite irrespective of any ideas I might have on the subject. He is unfortunately very one-paced and one day coming round the last bend at Sandown I pulled him sharply out to challenge the leaders in the hope of out-jumping them at the Pond. Unknown to me, unfortunately, David Mould had decided to make his effort at the same place and time—and in the collision which resulted his horse was knocked wide, losing ground which, in his eloquently expressed opinion, cost him victory.

One of the best and certainly one of the most stylish jockeys with whom I rode, David has always been a professional to his finger-tips and you could describe the extent of his admiration for amateur riders in large letters on a very small postage stamp. 'I never talk to bumpers except to say get out of the way,' he once remarked. However, this is not entirely true, because on the occasion described above he addressed me as follows: 'The only thing you ever had was a bit of a brain, you silly old fool,' he said, 'and now that's gone as well!'

I hasten to add that this story is not entirely typical of the relationship between amateur riders and professional jockeys—or between David and myself. Two weeks after the incident described above I followed him round the wide outside in a three-mile hurdle race when the mud was so deep near the inside rail that we both enjoyed a considerable advantage over our opponents. Between the last two flights I was able to overtake him (on account of having at least fourteen pounds in hand) and as we galloped past to victory the words 'you *cunning* old so-and-so' were music in my ears.

Left
Author John Oaksey (right), riding Cloudsmere, at the water jump on their way to second place in the Smith Lawns Handicap Chase at Windsor, January 1975

Jumping in fact is one of the very few sports nowadays in which the distinction between amateur and professional still not only exists but seems to serve a useful purpose. Of course it can easily be criticized as a 'snobbish', out-of-date survival; but the truth is that a very large number of men (and now women) would never taste the thrill of race riding over fences if it was not for the point-to-points (described elsewhere in this book), hunter chases, and amateur riders' races which remain an integral part of the British racing scene.

Some of them go on to become successful professional jockeys, some soldier on as amateurs and may end up as enthusiastic owners prepared to spend money they can probably ill afford in the search for the sort of horse they would have liked to ride.

But, professional or amateur, success or failure, they have all been bitten by the same bug which bit Messrs Blake and O'Callaghan all those years ago. Once you have asked a willing horse to jump a fence at speed you are never likely to forget his answer. And if that answer was a bold, clean leap which carried you both far out the other side you may find the memory difficult to replace. I have, anyway.

Steeplechasing in the United States

Jane Kidd

American steeplechasing has had surges in popularity and periods in the doldrums, and this has been reflected in variations in the total purse which has ranged, for example, from $350,000 to $190,000 within a single decade. The changes have been due to the number of steeplechasing showpiece activities, the jumping held at the major tracks, being periodically reduced; in some areas they have ended altogether. The governing body of steeplechasing, the National Steeplechase and Hunt Association (NS&HA), does however also supervise the jumping held at the Hunt Meetings. These are run and patronized by foxhunting-orientated folk, the main devotees of jumping, and their meetings have flourished since the end of the last century. This has ensured that the sport has kept going even when its more commercial and lucrative side was threatened.

Steeplechasing became popular in the USA long after it was established in the British Isles, its country of origin. The earliest recorded race over fences was at Hoboken, N.J., where a hurdle event was staged in 1844. The winner was Hops, which was not unexpected. He came from Canada where the Queens Own 7th Hussars had run the first Canadian jump race at their garrison in London, Ontario, during the previous year. It was another 20 years before records indicate a steeplechase being staged at a major American track, and this took the form of a three-mile handicap over 27 natural fences (walls, banks, timber, water etc). The venue was Paterson, N.J. in 1869 and a large crowd came to watch an unusually eventful race. Even the winner fell to be remounted, and the second, when he fell, damaged his rider so badly that a substitute jockey had to be found to take him over the remainder of the course.

A rather more formal venture was held four years later, as part of the race programme at Jerome Park. The public loved it and the steeplechase became an annual feature of Jerome Park's fall meeting. Other tracks, starting with Pimlico in Maryland in 1873, introduced their own steeplechase and the jumping became an established part of racing at the major American tracks.

This popular new sport was, like all forms of racing, dealt a hefty blow with the anti-betting legislation passed at the beginning of the century. Racing went through bleak times until some States later revised their puritanical laws. Flat racing revived in these betting States, as did steeplechasing, but for the latter there were more problems ahead. The 1940s brought the establishment of the *pari mutuel* system, and State after State (among those that allowed betting) introduced laws to run the bookmakers off the tracks.

This slowly changed the nature of the racing. The States took a percentage of the 'take', and their aim became the encouragement of betting in order to increase their income. The bettor was courted, more races put on for him; and the horse-lovers, those who came for the spectacle, were no longer catered for. The steeplechase, which so many of the latter enjoyed, was treated more and more as a non-commercial nuisance, especially as the gamblers were reluctant to invest their money in this race. They believed that the possibility of a horse falling was too great a hazard to the 'form', and no-one has yet convinced them that this is erroneous thinking; for in fact more favourites win over jumps than on the flat.

The track-operators, conscious of the lower 'take' in the steeplechase, reduced the numbers of events, until in 1971 the New York Racing Commission ended all jumping, except a little at Saratoga. It was a shattering blow to the sport.

The commissioners, however, were soon to discover they had made an error of judgement. Without the steeplechase their total betting 'take' fell. That amusing race in the middle of the eight- or ten-race programme added variety, and drew in more spectators who then contributed to the general pool.

Gradually courses re-introduced the steeplechase and today major tracks such as Delaware, Monmouth Park, Saratoga and Belmont Park run jumping meetings lasting for one to four weeks. On five days a week, during their racing season, one steeplechase is included in the race card. These races have large purses and the best steeplechasers collect from all over America to stable at the track, and train there for the duration of the jump meeting.

The American steeplechaser, however, leads a life of contrasts, as most of his races are run in very different atmospheres. The major tracks are the stage for the jumpers from June to August only, and during the colder parts of the year it is the Hunt Meets that provide the opportunity to earn perhaps less money but more glory. At these meetings the horse becomes a central feature again, as a means of creating 'sport', or proving the rider's courage and ability, and not merely as a medium for betting. Those interested in the betting are neglected, as official facilities are provided at one meeting only—Fair Hill, Md.

The closest most meetings come to organizing betting is with their 'Calcutta'. In this the horses in the major races are auctioned off to the highest bidder and the purchaser of the winner receives about 60 percent of the takings which can amount to as much as $30,000. The bidders are often caught in the best possible spirits, for the auction usually takes place at a party on the evening before the race. (It is described in greater detail in another chapter, page 101.) This time marks the opening of a weekend of merriment when owners, riders, trainers and friends collect in house-parties and celebrate the staging of the Hunt Meet with dinners, cocktail gatherings and usually a formal hunt ball after the race. For the local residents the race meeting is one of the social occasions of the year, for which many of them have worked voluntarily for months beforehand.

Spectators gather in large numbers—up to 30,000—at these unpretentious,

Below
Tommy Skiffington on Manco
Capac (right of picture) with
Still In All (ridden by his
owner Turney McKnight) in
the 1976 Middleburg Hunt
Cup at the Middleburg's
Glenwood Park course

informal sporting events. They can watch horses race on the flat, over timber, over brush, and even the ponies are given a special race at some meetings. A typical race-card will be one or two pony races, one or two flat races, one or two timber races and two or three brush races. Variety, entertainment and good sport are the keynotes of the occasion—how very different from the formal, commercial races which are squeezed in between the flat races at the major tracks.

These Hunt Meetings were started by foxhunters keen to make money for their hunts, or by sporting riders wanting to test fleet-footed hunters in a more competitive way than in the hunting-field. The first important one was started by the Western Long

Island foxhunters in 1883. For 60 years this meeting held one of the most important races in the USA—the Meadow Brook Cup—and it was only ended when the suburbs of New York spread to cover its ground. The Rose Tree, Philadelphia, and the Country Club at Brookline, Massachusetts, were others to organize important early Hunt Meets. Their races were all run over fair hunting fences, and in the USA for the most part there were and still are timber post-and-rails. They are not usually very high, about 3ft 6in (1m), and are often sloped, so that they are encouraging fences to race over at speed. The

timber races at the Hunt Meets today are not dissimilar to Britain's hurdle races, although they are a little more challenging as the fences are solid and slightly higher.

There has, however, grown up a circuit of Timber Races which are in a different domain from anything anywhere else in the world. The fences are not only high, up to 5ft 2in (1.60m), but also upright and solid; and racing over them at speed demands a clever, brilliant jumper and a courageous rider.

The Timber Race circuit has its origins in Maryland, where, towards the end of the last century, some gentlemen of the Elkridge Club began boasting about the merits of their respective hunters. They decided to test their steeds in a race over four miles of natural fences. On 26 May 1894 the first Maryland Hunt Cup was held. The race grew in stature, and was opened in 1903 to foreigners. The venue was changed in the early years, but since 1922 has been settled at Worthington Valley, Md., where the race is now run over grass. The plough, the wheatfields, the deep ditches and the fords are no longer part of the course, but the 22 stout post-and-rail and board fences, with one 6ft 3in (1.90m) brook, are stretched over four miles and provide a test that only the most sporting riders accept. The reward for the winner is mainly glory for, although a purse is now given, this hardly covers the costs of training the horse. No rider can be paid for competing, and it is only recently that those who earn money elsewhere from riding have been made eligible. The Maryland Hunt Cup has become one of the world's most truly sporting events.

Those training for it usually ride in the Pennsylvania Hunt Cup held in the fall, in the heart of the best American hunting country, at Unionville, Pa. Then in the spring there are the two three-mile races—the My Lady's Manor and the slightly stiffer course of the Grand National Point to Point. These two events lead up to the Maryland Hunt Cup and are run over three successive weekends. They are known as the Maryland Timber Classics. Few horses even enter all three, but that phenomenon Jay Trump actually won them all.

Those wanting to earn the more lucrative prizes must aim for the brush races. These are run over obstacles which are a good deal more forgiving than the timber post-and-rails, as on practically all the tracks synthetic obstacles are now used. In the past the fences were usually hurdles and fences packed with freshly cut cedar. These were expensive to rebuild each year and the governing body of American steeplechasing, the NS&HA, began experimenting with synthetic fences. In 1973 they finally tried out at the Fairfax fall meeting a modified version of the Irish prototype. There were no falls and track after track forwent their traditional obstacles to hire the easily transportable synthetic fences owned by the NS&HA.

The top half of synthetic brush fences can be jumped through, and they are not so high as the thick British steeplechase fences. The horses must therefore be quick rather than clean jumpers; and as they race mainly over relatively short distances, the need for speed rather than stamina and jumping ability becomes even more important. Some races are as short as $1\frac{1}{2}$ miles, and the steeplechasers' Triple Crown—the Grand National, the Temple Gwathmey and the Colonial Cup—are run over $2\frac{1}{2}$ miles, $2\frac{1}{2}$ miles and $2\frac{13}{16}$ miles respectively. The three-mile steeplechase is a rarity, and the only major ones are the Iroquois and Hardscuffle in May. The American brush jumper is a fleet-footed animal, as those from the home of steeplechasing have found out. Some of the

Opposite
A Hunt Meet in Virginia: Harvey L. Styer on his My Cat goes through the wing of a fence in the 1975 Casanova Point-to-Point, while Tim McGrath on Captain Carlo jumps without incident

Overleaf
Frank Chapot on Evening Mail coming over the 13th fence in the 1973 Maryland Hunt Cup. Buzz Hannum on Morning Mac leads on his way to victory.

cream of the horses from the British Isles and France have been slammed when they came over to challenge the Americans for their richest prize of the year—the Colonial Cup. When Grand Canyon finally took the spoils back across the Atlantic in 1976 his glories were tempered by the knowledge that the hosts could only field an unusually low standard of entries.

The Colonial Cup is held in November at the Camden, South Carolina meeting, and it marks the grand finale to the American steeplechasing season, a season which is almost entirely confined to the area east of the Mississippi. Let us follow it through the major meetings from the beginning. The activities start in the south in mid-March at the relatively new course of Atlanta in Georgia, and from then until the end of May avid steeplechasers may go to one- or two-day meetings every weekend. They are all held at permanent tracks, but with the exception of Camden (South Carolina), Fair Hill (Maryland) and Middleburg (Virginia), which have spring and fall meetings, these tracks are only used once a year.

For the followers of steeplechasing this entails a great deal of travelling, but the races are organized in circuits. The Dixie circuit starts the season, with the Atlanta opening followed by a few weeks in the Carolinas—at Aiken, then Camden and after this a little further north at the hilly course of Tryon at the foothills of the Blue Ridge mountains. Then they move across to the Southern Pines at Stoneybrook Farm, and to Tanglewood, Piedmont, where the course is part of a complete resort.

The steeplechasing scene then moves northwards to the home of the hard core of American foxhunters—the Virginias and Maryland; and it is here that the Timber Races become a major feature. Then in May the racing swings towards the Mid-west, with the Oxmoor, followed by the High Hope meeting at the Kentucky State Horse Park where facilities are springing up for every type of horse activity, including the cross country course for the 1978 Three Day Event World Championships. Then there is the Iroquois at Nashville which is one of the few tracks which still uses its own brush fences, and the Hardscuffle, one of the newest of the meetings. The spring season ends at Fair Hill, the course that William Du Pont, Jr. built over his estates in Maryland. It is the only track approaching the British type of race-track, as there are permanent facilities, stands and betting booths. It is, too, the only Hunt Meeting at which the State allows and organizes the betting.

June, July and August is the time for the more commercial form of steeplechasing, when the major tracks stage a season of one jump race a day. At these the professional approach prevails, and those favouring a day when steeplechasing dominates have to wait for the fall season which opens where the spring closed, at Fair Hill. The action then passes to the new course of Fairfax at the historic Belmont Plantation near Leesburg, Va. After this there is the lucrative Rolling Rock meeting which is held in a vast park run as a club where members have their own foxhunt, golf and numerous other sporting facilities. Their special entertainment in October, however, is a two-day Hunt Meeting. Then there is Middleburg, Far Hill, N.J., and Montpelier, where the beautiful home of President Madison provides an elegant backcloth to the proceedings. Finally, it is time for Camden and the only international race of the year—the Colonial Cup.

After this, all that remains for American steeplechasers is the presentation of their

Opposite
Turning for home in a hurdle race at the Fair Hill steeplechase course in Maryland

awards, and there is a small band of names that tends to monopolize these. The leading trainer has since 1973 been the young Englishman, Jonathan Sheppard, whose father was the British Jockey Club's senior handicapper. Jonathan Sheppard gave up an establishment career as a London stockbroker to toy with racing in the USA. He started by riding, took out a trainer's licence in 1966, and now seems to be achieving the sort of domination of the training honours that 'Mike' Smithwick held before him (he won the title twelve times).

The jockey honours have fluctuated recently between Jerry Fishback, who first started riding with the Pony Club, and Tom Skiffington, who has spent an entire season and a number of winter sojourns riding in Britain and France. To win the jockey title these professionals ride between 20 and 40 winners, which are mainly over jumps, but the odd victory in a flat race at a Hunt Meet is also included. The amateur title normally falls to 'Kip' Elser who is good enough to get more rides than most of the professionals. He is usually pressed closest by the winner of this title in 1970—George Sloan, the Tennessee businessman who commutes across the Atlantic to ride winners in the UK as well.

The successful owners are a small, élite band of rich patrons—the Mellons, the Guests, the Valentines, the Ogden Phippses; venerable people whose names have figured as leading owners on both sides of the Atlantic. Junior to them is the owner who in most recent years has found the key to winning both the largest amount of prize money and the largest total of winners. He is the university professor George Strawbridge, Jr., who has been a top amateur rider himself. His horses race in the green and white silks of his Augustin Stables, and are trained predominantly by the champion Jonathan Sheppard.

The honour of owning the Champion Steeplechaser of the year has, however, fallen to others. Virginia Van Alen, the daughter of Raymond Guest, the Chairman of the NS&HA and owner of L'Escargot, dual winner of Britain's Cheltenham Gold Cup and Grand National, became the 1975 first lady of steeplechasing as owner of Life's Illusion. Mrs Miles Valentine, who owns many horses run on the British jumping tracks too, has also achieved this honour as owner of the Colonial Cup winner Lucky Boy II. Mrs Ogden Phipps, wife of an ex-Chairman of the Jockey Club, is another leading patron who has won many awards including most recently the 1976 Eclipse Award (champion horse voted for by the turf writers) with Straight and True. Mrs Marion Du Pont Scott, the Colonial Cup sponsor, is one of the few to breed steeplechasers specifically and these include the top stakes winner of all time, Neji ($271,956). Soothsayer is another of her horses, but she also encourages those starting steeplechasing by selling them some of her young stock.

American steeplechasing is an expensive sport. The travelling and training costs are high and the opportunities to win rewards limited. This means that it is dominated by the rich and the professionals; but for those who are unable to give as much money and time to racing there is the point-to-point. The point-to-point season starts and finishes earlier than that of the NS&HA-sanctioned meetings, running from mid-February to mid-April.

The events put on are so various that practically anybody wanting to try racing over not-very-high fences can find an opportunity. Some of the more unusual races frequently included are the owner-rider races, heavyweight races, junior flat races and hunting pair

races which might be run over a flagged course of hunting country. Even in the more 'establishment'-type races, the maiden, lady, and gentleman riders can if they wish don hunting attire rather than racing silks.

The point-to-point is what it was originally intended to be: an informal race for foxhunters. Although thoroughbred horses predominate, field hunters are found amongst the starters. There is growing anxiety, however, that professionalism is creeping in, as some meetings no longer impose the condition that all entries must have been fairly hunted; and money as well as a trophy is being offered in some races.

At present the more serious steeplechasers do use the point-to-points as schooling-grounds or warm-up sessions for the sanctioned racing. The most prized point-to-points—the Cheshire Bowl at Unionville, Pa., the Howard County Cup at Glenelg, Md., and the Rokeby Bowl at Piedmont, Va.—are over relatively stiff courses and are usually won by good horses that go on to do well in sanctioned races.

The point-to-point was said to have been started in America in 1859 by the Rose Tree Foxhunting Club close to Philadelphia, Pa. Since then the organization of each event has been entirely in the hands of the particular hunt concerned, which can impose its own rules. Consequently the fences that are raced over (mainly timber), the conditions of the races, and the prizes offered vary enormously.

One thing is certain though—the total number of point-to-points is increasing, and this may be associated with the growth in the numbers of hunts. After the last war there were less than 100 official hunts and now there are close to 150.

This increase in the number of hunts also augurs well for the Hunt Meetings as most of these, like the point-to-points, are used to replenish their hunt's coffers. Most years one or two new Hunt Meetings are added to the calendar, some developing out of point-to-points, and others like the High Hope meeting at the Kentucky State Park being part of extensive projects to build up a general sporting centre. The number of participants is increasing. Only 250 horses raced over Hunt Meeting fences in 1972 but the figure is now rising, although it has not reached the best times when there were 500 steeplechasers.

However much the Hunt Meets prosper, the key to a truly successful jumping game lies with the support given to it by the major tracks, the general public and bettors; and not just a small band of foxhunters and jumping devotees. The track organizers have learnt the lesson that the removal of steeplechasing from their season reduces rather than increases their betting 'take', but there is still a need for more races and better public relations. With only a few races on the tracks and practically no television, the layman does not become familiar with the sport; and it is not until towards the end of the season on the major tracks that there is any form to use for betting. With no gambling at the Hunt Meetings, and the varying standards of their courses, it is difficult for them to provide genuine form.

It seems unlikely that steeplechasing in the USA can expand steadily unless the major source of revenue—the bettor—is given a better understanding of the sport, more information and greater encouragement to invest. If this does not happen, however, it is likely that American steeplechasing will continue to be a very friendly activity which gives pleasure to a relatively small but sporting and enthusiastic group of people.

Previous page
Mrs Ogden Phipps's Straight and True (with hood) (jockey Jerry Fishback) taking the last fence in the 1976 Grand National at Fair Hill, Maryland. He won this race en route to the title of Steeplechaser of the Year.

Opposite above
Great going in the Ladies' Race at the 1977 Blue Ridge Point-to-Point

Opposite below
Turney McKnight on Hammurabi (centre), Charles Fenwick on Venture II (left) and Olympic medallist Bruce Davidson on Danny's Brother (right) in the Benjamin H. Murray Memorial race at Butler, Maryland, in 1975

A British Jockey in the Colonial Cup
Philip Blacker

South Carolina and the Colonial Cup could hardly have been further from my mind, as I was riding-out one miserable November morning at trainer Alan Jarvis's Coventry stable, in the heart of England.

Out on the gallops, the three-year-old in my charge had clearly decided that he had hung about in the cold for long enough, and was performing a series of violent contortions in a determined bid to unseat me; mercifully the trainer's arrival, and his prescribed piece of fast-work over seven furlongs, averted disaster, since the gallop provided an ample outlet for the horse's excess energy.

Half an hour later, 15 steaming racehorses were being led round to cool off before returning to the comfort of their stables.

'Oh, Philip, John Edwards's wife rang while you were riding-out. Wants you to call her back when you get in,' Mr Jarvis informed me as he scrutinized each animal individually. John had been successfully training a string of about 35 horses in the county of Herefordshire for seven years, and I was one of the several jockeys he employed from time to time. As his wife, Gina, answered my call, I was fully expecting her to inquire into my riding plans the following day at Wolverhampton, where the Edwards's stable runners were engaged. Instead she said, 'Can you fly out to Camden in South Carolina within the next few days to ride High Ken in the Colonial Cup on 15 November?' She went on to explain that the horse's regular jockey, Barry Brogan, had elected to stay at home to ride the much fancied Flashy Boy in the Black and White Chase at Ascot the same day.

High Ken was at this time the star of the Edwards's stable, and, as a result of winning some good-class races the previous season, was one of the several foreign horses invited by the Colonial Cup committee to compete for the $50,000 purse. First held in 1970 to celebrate South Carolina's bi-centenary, the race was the brainchild of Mrs Marion DuPont Scott on whose estate Springdale racecourse lies. Former amateur rider Ray Woolfe, who was manager of the racecourse then, persuaded 70 other 'chasing enthusiasts to put up several thousand dollars apiece to sponsor the race, which was to be run over 2 miles and 6 furlongs, and 18 fences. Having put up the prize-money, the sponsors then invited ten of the best foreign jumpers in training to compete.

Furthermore, the committee undertook to pay all the travelling and living expenses of the horses, grooms, trainers and jockeys who accepted the challenge from abroad. Their aim was to make the Colonial Cup a truly international steeplechase by inviting the best 'chasers in Europe to take on the cream of North America. However, in this, the 1975 running of the race, High Ken from England, and Captain Christy (winner of Britain's Cheltenham Gold Cup and King George VI Cup), representing Ireland, were the only foreigners in the line-up.

Despite the fact that the English hope was considered an outsider to win the race, I immediately decided that, provided I could get the go-ahead from my two retainers to be away for a week, this was an opportunity not to be missed. Soon I was back on the line to Gina Edwards to say I could fly out to South Carolina on 11 November to join the horse and his trainer, who were already in Camden preparing for the race.

A violent storm greeted me as my plane touched down at last at Columbia airport in South Carolina; but if I felt a certain amount of relief at reaching my destination, I can imagine that my Colonial Cup partner, arriving at Camden nine days earlier, had felt a great deal more than that. High Ken and his handler, amateur rider Chris Crozier, had embarked for America exactly a fortnight before. But their five-day-long journey was not without its hitches, which left the horse drained of energy.

Although aware of the American quarantine regulations, Chris could feel nothing but concern when, on their arrival at New York, High Ken was removed from his charge and loaded into a truck and driven away to an unknown destination. After some enquiries, he located the pound in which the horse was to remain for the next two days, but was then informed that on no account was he to go anywhere near the animal, let alone see to his welfare. The animal that finally emerged from the quarantine pound bore little resemblance to the one that Chris had handed over a couple of days before. No doubt the unfamiliar surroundings and strange food contributed to the horse's loss of weight and dejected appearance. Anyway, with his morale at a low ebb already, the following day he was to embark on a long and arduous journey by truck to the Deep South, and ironically Captain Christy, who was known to be a more highly strung character, joined his English companion at Belmont Park that evening after enduring his period in quarantine with stoic resilience. The next day the two horses were loaded up and set off by road for South Carolina, and thirty hours later the exhausted travellers arrived at Camden after a non-stop, 700-mile journey.

It was not surprising that by this time the English challenger did not, at first sight anyway, instil an enormous amount of fear into the hearts of his American opponents. Indeed, High Ken's 'tucked-up' figure, drooping head and listless expression caused one unkind observer to advise Chris, who was grooming the horse at the time, not to brush *too* hard as he might keel over. However, 'the Captain' had taken the long trek surprisingly well, and after a day or two in Camden appeared relaxed and at home. They had only a fortnight in which to prepare and acclimatize for the race, and in High Ken's case this seemed precious little time.

After the storm that was raging on my arrival at Camden I was pleased to see, on being dragged from my bed by John Edwards early the next morning, that the rain had subsided, replaced by a clear and sunny but sharply cold day. At 8.30am our car, lent to us by courtesy of the Colonial Cup committee, pulled up at a small wooden building at

Previous page
Raymond Guest's The
Bo-Weevil ridden by Tommy
Stack (nearest to camera) in the
1976 Colonial Cup, landing
over the first fence

Below
Mrs Marion Dupont Scott
presents winning jockey Ron
Barry with his trophy at the
1976 Colonial Cup

one extremity of Springdale racecourse, and Pat Taaffe and Bobby Coonan, Captain Christy's trainer and jockey respectively, accompanied by John Edwards and myself, bundled out. This is the Colonial Cup office, and the nerve-centre of the whole production run by Dale Thiel, the race organizer, and his few dedicated helpers. From this vantage point the Carolina pines, which encompass most of the course, open up to provide a superb view of the track, which absorbs a huge acreage and is as flat as a billiard-table. But it is certainly not as green as one, for the turf growing out of the sandy soil looks brown and parched. The going is not as firm as one would think at first, though, as the sandy terrain does provide a little much-needed cushion for a horse's fragile limbs.

However, the grandstand by the finishing straight is not proportionately expansive, being large enough to hold only a tiny percentage of the many thousands of racegoers. This is far from being due to any reluctance on Mrs DuPont Scott's part to build a bigger one, but merely because most spectators prefer to watch the sport from their cars,

parked in the centre of the course for maximum visibility. For me, as an Englishman, this created a point-to-point-like atmosphere which belied the fact that thousands of dollars were at stake throughout the afternoon.

But I did not need reminding of the high stakes when Captain Christy and High Ken emerged from the stable-block reserved for the foreign horses, and Bobby and I were legged up on to our respective mounts before embarking on a schooling session over the American-style fences.

Adjacent to the course itself is the training and schooling ground, where several of our big-race opponents were already being put through their paces. The cluster of owners and trainers assembled in the centre of this area watched with interest as we advanced upsides on the first of the half-dozen schooling fences. John had been unable to hide his anxiety as we were about to set off, and could not restrain himself from imploring me not to fall off in front of everyone. I laughingly told him to show some confidence in his jockey, but quietly dropped my leathers another two holes, just to be on the safe side. He need not have worried. Both animals performed satisfactorily, jumping perhaps a shade too deliberately. The Colonial Cup fences are in fact rather similar in size and shape to those in Britain. However, the brushwood which comprises the top half of the 4ft 6in (1.37m) obstacle is loosely packed and easily dislodged. Consequently horses used to jumping the stiffer, birch-packed British fences tend to waste too much time in the air until they become aware that such care is unnecessary.

With the introduction of plastic, portable fences now in general use in the States, permanent obstacles made from natural materials are rarely used. Plastic fences are regarded as the saviour of jump racing in America since they require nothing like the maintenance of the normal ones. What is more, at the end of each meeting they can be loaded onto a truck and driven to the next venue, saving thousands of dollars in the process. Their base is covered with a thick layer of foam rubber to protect a horse's legs from the metal frame on the inside, while the top half consists of a plastic hedge closely resembling birchwood. All the jumping races at Camden, other than the Colonial Cup, are run over these obstacles, which are erected on a separate track inside that used for the big race.

With High Ken safely back in the hands of Chris Crozier, I was able to take a closer look at the rest of the activity on the training ground.

The American trainer Mikey Smithwick was exercising his entry for the big race, the French horse Straight and True, for whom he had secured the services of top Irish jockey Tommy Carberry. Tommy had accepted the ride in preference to a slightly less fancied runner, Café Prince. The Irish champion, who had ridden in every previous Colonial Cup so far with only one success, was to live to regret that decision.

Having watched the rest of the coming Saturday's runners receiving varying degrees of work, we adjourned to the nearby Colonial Cup office, where Dale Thiel handed us a cup of coffee, and read out the latest show of betting just received from New York. Apparently every patriotic Irishman in the state was backing Captain Christy 'like he was the biggest certainty ever to look through a bridle', causing the New York bookies to slash his odds to 3 to 1. Second in the betting at 5 to 1 came the 1972 winner, Soothsayer. Because of the State of South Carolina's strict non-gambling laws, all betting transactions and price quotes have to be operated from New York. Despite this inconvenience, about half a million dollars was laid on the Colonial Cup in the twelve hours before the race.

Cocktail parties and social functions came thick and fast in the days leading up to the race, and at the inevitable lunch-time drinks party held the day before it, one topic of conversation dominated the rest.

Chris 'Kip' Elser and Leo O'Brien, two prominent jockeys in the States, were among those discussing their big-race chances. 'Kip' is officially among the amateur ranks, but in fact gets as many rides in public as most of the top professionals, and easily holds his own among them. O'Brien seemed quietly confident about the chances of his mount, Gran Kan. The room buzzed with rumours about the fancied runners. One particular report concerned Soothsayer, who was said to have worked 'like a flying machine' earlier in the week.

On the eve of the Colonial Cup each year, a party is held in a marquee erected behind the grandstand on the racecourse. The high spot of the evening is an auction, during which all the runners in the big race are 'sold'. In fact, what each successful bidder buys is a chance to claim 55 percent of the total amount raised at the auction if his horse wins the race. The successful bidder of the second horse receives 30 percent, the third takes 10 percent and the fourth five.

The purpose of the auction is two-fold. Firstly, it boosts the race funds, since 10 percent of the total is taken for this purpose; secondly, it provides an opportunity for several wealthy people to make a substantial wager, without infringing the state's no-betting laws. I say 'wealthy people', because bidding can go up to several thousand dollars for any one of the more fancied runners. By the end of the evening $25,950 had been raised. Michael O'Hehir excelled himself as auctioneer, coaxing a top bid of $4000 out of ex-champion flat-race jockey Eddie Acaro for Captain Christy. Soothsayer (who had finished second in the Cheltenham Gold Cup that year) fetched $3100, while Virginia Van Alen's Life's Illusion went to Mrs Miles Valentine for $2600.

Unfortunately there was no such enthusiasm when High Ken's turn came to go under the hammer. Despite O'Hehir's urgings, no-one seemed anxious to invest in his chances. Mrs Richard Hickman, wife of the horse's owner, decided that *some* confidence must be shown by the animal's connections if no-one else, and tentatively raised her finger with the intention of opening the bidding at $100. O'Hehir seized upon Mrs Hickman's raised hand with such undisguised glee that he misinterpreted her gesture as a bid for one *thousand* dollars and proceeded to knock the horse down to her for that amount. Since the bidding for most of the eighteen runners had opened at $1000 or more, his mistake was understandable, but this was small consolation to Richard Hickman who viewed the proceedings with an expression of mute disbelief.

Michael O'Hehir continued to 'sell' the remainder of the runners, including the 1974 winner of the race, Augustus Bay, who was in big demand, as was the same year's Jumper of the Year, Gran Kan.

By mid-morning the next day, Springdale racecourse had become a hive of activity. I arrived early, and after dumping my kit in the tent provided, which was to serve as jockeys' changing- and weighing-room, I walked out on to the course to reassure myself that I was totally familiar with it. The car park in the centre was already full, and emerging from every car was an endless flow of liquid refreshment and all manner of

culinary delights. Fortunately the sunny, warm day enabled the racegoers to enjoy their picnic in the open.

The first race of the day was a $5000 handicap chase named in memory of Ray Woolfe, Mrs DuPont Scott's trainer and racecourse manager, who had died in August of that year. This was won by the highly successful partnership of owner Mrs Miles Valentine and her trainer Burling Cocks, with the able assistance of stable jockey, Tommy Skiffington. 'Skiff' went on to wind up the day and the season in great style by completing a treble, leaving him as runner-up in the jockeys' table behind champion Jerry Fishback.

The British system of providing valets in the jockeys' changing room to cater for their every whim had left me disorganized, to say the least, when I was left to my own devices. Breastplates, weightcloths, wither pads and all the other paraphernalia that accompanies a racing saddle lay in confusion at one corner of the tent, while I tried to borrow some small pieces of essential equipment, omitted from my bag on the misconception that wherever there was a jockeys' changing room, there just had to be a valet! Eventually I emerged correctly attired from the changing tent, with the other jockeys, and walked the short distance through the pine trees to the parade ring.

Captain Christy strutted round the paddock like a true champion, but sporting a winter coat, which had grown quite alarmingly since leaving Ireland. High Ken seemed to be taking the proceedings completely in his stride, and appeared to be almost *too* indifferent to his surroundings. Augustus Bay looked in peak condition, and with the man in form on board, Tommy Skiffington, the combination looked to be as big a threat as anything in the race.

The dejected-looking trio standing next to our group in the paddock had every right to believe that this was not their day. Disaster had struck in the very first race for the trainer, who had seen his promising three-year-old fall and suffer a fatal injury. In the saddle at the time had been the jockey now talking to him, and discreetly massaging his shoulder to prevent it from stiffening after his heavy fall. The second race brought disappointment to the third member of the trio. He had just ridden another of his own horses in an amateur-riders' flat-race—and finished last. So as the owner of Café Prince, George Strawbridge, watched his trainer, Jonathan Sheppard, leg up the aching Dave Washer into the saddle, I would not have been surprised if he had been recalling the saying that bad luck often occurs in runs of three.

Out on the course the 18 runners were paraded in front of the crowd before being released by their handlers to canter down to the start. High Ken had at last begun to display some enthusiasm and, as Chris slipped the lead rein from the bridle and wished us luck, the horse grabbed hold of his bit and broke into a swinging canter.

My concern at this point was the unfamiliar method of starting used in the race. Instead of the barrier start to which I was accustomed in England, here the runners circle round next to the track until the order is given to file out on to the course. One behind the other they walk until the whole field is positioned so that the two starting posts are situated at the ends of the column. At the starter's signal, each jockey is required to turn his mount at a right-angle, so facing up the course, and head for the first fence. Luckily a film-show of previous Colonial Cups, laid on by Dale Thiel two days earlier, had clearly demonstrated the need to be familiar with these proceedings.

Opposite
Author Philip Blacker on High Ken (next to riderless horse) in the 1975 Colonial Cup

Whatever occurred during the race, I was determined not to get left. So as the starter dropped his flag, I abruptly pulled High Ken round to his right, gave him a kick in the ribs, and we were away among the leaders.

The Colonial Cup has a reputation for being run at breakneck speed, so the plan was to jump High Ken sharply out of the gate, in order to get established in a handy position just behind the leaders. This all went according to plan, and we were able to settle in on the inside. Upsides me early on was Bobby Coonan and 'the Captain', clearly following the same tactics as ourselves. It did not take long before High Ken discovered to his satisfaction that he could treat the 18 identical obstacles with a certain lack of respect and still get away with it. However, this was no bad thing, since economical jumping was essential for holding one's position in the blistering pace being set.

With three-quarters of a mile to run, the cracking gallop set by Life's Illusion began to tell on my mount. Upsides me, Bobby was still sitting against Captain Christy with a tight rein.

Four fences from home I knew we were beaten. As several of the runners moved up to challenge the leading group, I shouted across to Coonan, 'Go on, Bobby, you're going to trot up!' At that point he released a couple of inches of rein and 'the Captain' shrugged us off with an electrifying burst of speed that sent him up to the front in a few strides.

Turning for home with two fences to jump, 'the Captain' went clear, hotly pursued by Augustus Bay, Soothsayer, Café Prince and the tiring Life's Illusion.

The Camden fences may be soft, but for Captain Christy they certainly needed to be, for at the second last he made an appalling blunder that totally demolished his section of the fence, and left a hole that would have done credit to a tank. Miraculously he stood up, but the encounter had knocked the stuffing out of him. Running to the final fence, the gallant Captain still held the lead, but Café Prince, Augustus Bay and Soothsayer were on his heels like a pack of hungry wolves bearing down on their exhausted quarry. On the run for home Dave Washer called up every resource available to Café Prince, and forged past the Irish horse with Augustus Bay in pursuit. In that order they passed the post, with Soothsayer just getting up to deprive Captain Christy of third position. Café Prince's three-length win ensured for Jonathan Sheppard the championship title for the third successive season.

As for High Ken, the turn of speed displayed by many of our opponents in the last half-mile, plus very fast going and a race rather short of his best distance, had finally relegated us to tenth place. Our race was put in a nutshell by the description one American jockey gave of his own mount's performance—'We were going great until we turned into the home stretch, and then they came past me so fast my goggles flew off in the slipstream!'

With the business side of the day dispensed with, the close of the 1975 jumping season in America was celebrated in fine style.

The jockeys' annual end-of-season dance held at the Camden Shrine Club was an event not to be missed. Certainly all those connected with the 'chasing scene in America seemed to think so, as the majority of them were there.

Captain Christy's owner, Mrs Jane Samuel, with the tension of the last few days released, was taking her horse's defeat with commendable sportsmanship, and at one

Opposite
The climax of the hunter chase season in England, the *Horse and Hound* Final Hunter Chase Championship at Stratford-upon-Avon. Just in the picture on the extreme right, wearing the white cap, is the young amateur rider Joey Newton, riding Credit Call, who went on to win the race.

Opposite
American Olympic gold medal
combination Denny Emerson
and Victor Deakin at the 1976
Middletown Olympic
Screening Trials

point in the evening she announced her intention to be back for a return fight next year. Tommy Carberry was not allowing the depressing thought that he had turned down the ride of Café Prince in favour of Straight and True (who never figured in the race at all) mar his enjoyment. John Edwards thoughtfully decided that a few words of gratitude to the Colonial Cup organizers would be appropriate, and echoed all our sentiments in his short speech, adding that it would not take much to persuade him to return next year, provided he could find a faster horse.

In the small hours of the morning, one ebullient American jockey bounced up to me and announced loudly, 'Well, Phil, maybe we didn't let ya ride a winner here, but we'll sure as hell get ya laid!' As he disappeared once again into the crowd on the dance-floor to find me a likely candidate, I resigned myself to the idea that the 7am flight to New York would leave without this particular booked passenger aboard!

Despite catching a later-than-planned flight to New York the following day, I calculated that with luck my connection flight would arrive at Heathrow on Monday in time for me to drive to Leicester races, where I had several booked rides. During my journey I wondered how long it would be before a British effort took the Colonial Cup. The horse required to win the race would have to be a tough, fast, staying hurdler. The British chasers rely too much on their jumping ability, which is not at a premium at Camden.

One year later, English trainer Derek Kent was to find the formula for success with Mr Pat Samuel's immensely resilient New Zealand-bred hurdler, Grand Canyon; powerfully assisted by Irish-born jockey, Ron Barry, they took the race by half a length. Filling the position taken by Captain Christy the year before came another British challenger, Lanzarote. He too was in with a fighting chance in the last half of the race, but a bad mistake at the final fence threw away his chance. The victorious Grand Canyon and his elated connections returned to England in a blaze of glory. Ex-champion jockey Ron Barry was naturally over the moon about his successful trip, and the fun-loving Irishman was still smiling when I saw him at the races a day or two later. I asked him what he thought of racing in North America. He grinned.

'Jeez, it's a great gas, isn't it!'

Jump Racing in the French Countryside

Ivor Herbert

Opposite above
A nineteenth-century engraving of a French military steeplechase

Opposite below
The Steeple-Chase-Cross-Country Prix Georges du Breil at Craon, 1976. Ukraine III (foreground), ridden by M. A. Jouenne, won the race.

'Several horses and one jockey killed here recently.' The dapper, youngish man in the tweed coat, cavalry-twill trousers and small tight tweed cap nods at one spot of the sandy turf close to the Mediterranean Sea. He speaks in French, for this is M. de Premerelle, who used to farm and breed horses in Morocco under French rule. He is now the capable racecourse manager of the luxurious Hippodrome of the Côte d'Azur.

Behind his back (French racing folk favour English-style clothes) the Bay of Angels is splashed across the horizon, in a painter's wash of aquamarine, stippled in gold. It is January. Circles of primulas and pansies hem the neat umbrella pines. The sun this morning is still a few hours from its zenith. But it is warm. When it goes down beyond Cap d'Antibes after racing at Cagnes-sur-Mer, the sea will flame off Nice towards the Italian frontier, and it will feel in the dusk as nippy as an English September evening.

But there are flowers not only on the ground, but in the air. Pale mimosa in bursts of misty lemon festoons the trees. French mid-winter steeplechasing is a fragrant escape. The sunlight streams through 'The Brook' which claimed its recent victims. The Brook at Cagnes is an obstacle towards the eastern end (where the blocks of apartments start) of the complicated junctions of the circuit.

There is no water in The Brook. It is an artificial hollow. The real river, which flows down the western side of this exceptionally pretty yet suburban racecourse, is the Loup. Its waters are used to irrigate the jumping, flat and inner trotting tracks.

The jump called The Brook comprises three thick and solid white rails, fixed to stout uprights resembling part of a millionaire's stud fencing. It is placed on the top edge of an upward-sloping, grass bank. Below the rails the lines of the posts continue into the scooped-out hollow in the turf from which the obstacle gets its name.

It bears as little resemblance to an English or Irish steeplechase fence as do nearly all the terrifying jumps at Badminton or Burghley. As such, British steeplechase fans may view it derisively. But it is *less* unlike the natural obstacles first encountered in original church steeple-to-steeple cross-country riding than are the regimented, black, artificial birch fences of race-tracks in Britain and Ireland. The variety of weird obstacles on French steeplechase tracks—and particularly in those races designated 'St-Ch C.C.' (standing for steeplechase cross-country)—are in fact less artificial than Britain's uniform, tough, birch jumps.

Some of the French jumps are certainly flimsier. It is this inconsistency which makes them dangerous to untutored foreign horses. Others, like The Brook and The Wall at Cagnes-sur-Mer, are solidly built and unbreakable. They will be taken moreover at racing speed by generally lightweight jockeys on slim-built horses.

The pace of nearly every French jumping race is strong from the start. Steeplechase fields are seldom three- or four-horse affairs: 10 to 17 turn out for most races at Cagnes. There is thus little dawdling. The winner is seldom waited with, but comes nine times out of ten from the bunch which has cut out the work from flag-fall. Stalls are not used, but the starts are neither noisier, more excited nor more ragged than those in Britain.

The immense complexity of Cagnes-sur-Mer resembles in plan a layout for a sophisticated model-railway circuit. There are two separate loops to the east of the main left-handed circuit. The space between the middle and the inner loop is bisected both ways by tracks in a St Andrew's Cross, so that the direction of general travel round the course may be altered. This is a common enough practice in Continental jump racing, though unheard of in the British Isles. Twisting complicated tracks, underlining the close link between French jump racing and cross country riding, are typical of the country.

The *existence* of racing at Nantes on the Atlantic coast is unknown to most English, yet it is closer to most of them than Scotland. Twenty-five meetings are held a year there at the Hippodrome du Petit-Port. The two principal steeplechases of 4300 metres each are races of £7000 ($11,970) and £13,800 ($23,598) and run in May and October.

The big hurdle race, the Grande Course des Haies, over 3900 metres is another £7000 ($11,970) race in May. The 5000-metre Nantes Grand Steeple-Chase-Cross-Country takes place in November and is worth £5750 ($9,833). So is their Prix du Prince, a big hurdle for three-year-olds over 3100 metres which takes place at November's end.

At Nantes there is basically a circuit plus one loop for the left-handed hurdle track, but there exist four different *'parcours'* for the *'steeples'*, and yet another with up to 28 obstacles for the cross country.

On France's other and warmer sea coast I ask M. de Premerelle at Cagnes-sur-Mer how jockeys can trace their way around as races switch from one *parcours* to another. Dolling-off to divert runners from the wrong tracks (such as exists on the run-in on some British courses) is negligible in France. The Côte d'Azur manager regards me with surprise: 'There are maps in the weighing-room.'

We walk on round the flat circuit. It is Saturday morning, a blank day in the six-week jumping season which begins in mid-December and concludes at the end of January with the Grand Prix de la Ville de Nice. This is a 4500-metre condition steeplechase for five-year-olds and up, minimum weight 62kg with penalties raising the weights up to 71kg. It is a plate of £27,660 ($47,300). Of this the winner takes £14,634 ($25,024) plus a *'prime'* of £1756 ($3000) for his breeder. This total value puts the race at only £200 less than Cheltenham's Piper Champagne Gold Cup—the classic race of Britain's jumping year.

All races at Cagnes, as generally elsewhere throughout France, carry prizes down to fourth place and all carry in addition the special *'primes'* for breeders. The main races carry an extra bonus, usually of a further 10 percent to the owners—another *'prime'*.

The four-year-old novice hurdle over 3000 metres preceding the Grand Prix de la Ville de Nice was, except for the £2765 ($4728) selling steeplechase (*'St-Ch. A réclamer'* in French), the least valuable race on the card of the 20th day of a recent winter season. The proportions in which its prize money and *'primes'* are divided are representative of the French system. The four-year-old hurdle, the Prix de Cimiez, with a total value of Frs. 37,800 (£4609 or $7881) was split thus: Frs. 20,000 to the winner plus a Frs. 2400 *'prime'*, Frs. 8000 to the second plus 10 percent *'prime'*, Frs. 4000 to the third plus 10 percent and Frs. 2000 to the fourth plus the 10 percent Frs. 200 *'prime'*. To finish fourth in a novice hurdle at Cagnes a horse thus gains about £270 ($462) . . . not much less than his British equivalent earns for *winning* a comparable race on an English provincial track.

M. de Premerelle and I continue round the course. The ground is loose and sandy and, towards the end of the winter jumping season when roughly scourged by many hooves, gives a false impression that it has become heavy. The soil is, however, too light

Below
A moment in the Grand Cross-Country at Craon, 1976

to become holding. Even on soft ground—and it does occasionally rain heavily in the South of France (vertical deluges, briefly descending on the oranges)—the horses move easily through it.

The water-jump in front of the elegant glass-sided grandstand (not unlike a smaller Sandown Park, but built in 1960) has a much higher but also thinner fence in front of it than the British variety. The water is as wide and the landing bank is shelved as steeply as British ones used to be, causing plenty of falls. There were two falls at the water-jump, la Rivière, in every steeplechase at a recent Cagnes-sur-Mer meeting.

The obstacles would pose no difficulty to any experienced eventer, such as David Nicholson's old Kildagin who won the Grand Steeplechase des Flandres up at Waregem in Belgium. But the pace at which the Cagnes steeplechases are run would leave 95 percent of event horses toiling. The 5 percent of exceptions would include the Chris Collins type of ex-racehorse, and Merely-a-Monarch, who before winning Badminton for Anneli Drummond-Hay had trounced two of the author's good hurdlers in a winding-up gallop.

British hurdlers would, however, cast dubious eyes and propping forelegs towards French steeplechase obstacles. There are vertical walls topped by a misleading crest of green privet. The open ditch at Cagnes is as wide as the British 'regulation' and the fence is as high. But it is considerably thinner. There are also two tall 'Bullfinches', one larger than the other and taller than the record height of a show jump. The intrepid horses must perforce hurtle through these; there is sufficient daylight to encourage a sensible jumper to do so.

The present course at Cagnes-sur-Mer was originally both a golf course and the scene of some of the earliest cross country events. Nearly all the stewards at Cagnes-sur-Mer are horsemen, most are retired cavalry officers (three were at Saumur, the crack cavalry school) and one recalls jumping into and out of the river Loup by the side of the present track and galloping about through a forest of pines on the slopes behind the present racecourse. Now those slopes are covered by blocks of expensive apartments which gaze down across the racecourse's green and golden 150 acres towards the flashing sea.

Upper-middle class flat horses easily win hurdle races at Cagnes. The hurdles take little jumping: a proper leap wastes time. They are made of tooth-brush tufts of old heather loosely packed into wooden frames like window-boxes. They are vertical, which does not encourage spectacular parabolas, thin, and dark-brown in colour. Hurdle winners at Cagnes are invariably light-built, whippy, flat-race types, capable of handling the sharp bends at the track's ends. Yet French jockeys surprisingly seldom favour going the shortest way. The early speed of the contests should enable horses to be waited with and tucked in. But the fields fan out round all the bends, and come down the finishing straight spread all across it from rail to rail like the charge of the lancers at Waterloo.

Cagnes-sur-Mer provides no less than 700 boxes in different yards on the track, a lads' hostel putting many a British country motel to shame, sand gallops and trotting tracks and schooling areas. Pressure on boxes is immense, because most horses spend the entire jumping season (and some the ensuing flat race season) down at Cagnes. Sometimes there are four applications per box, and new stabling with gallops is being constructed to the west on what was once the old racecourse at Cannes.

A good jumper, an experienced French trainer told the author, winning one race (not a major one) and being placed a couple of times should collect between £3500 ($5985) and £5500 ($9405) over the full six-week stay. Foreign horses are received a fortnight before the jumping starts in mid-December to afford time for the essential schooling. The most experienced English jump jockey at Cagnes by far is Martin Blackshaw, steeplechasing's equivalent of Tony Murray.

Cagnes-sur-Mer is a far, though melodious, cry from Newton Abbot; it is more like Sandown-by-Sea. Even so it falls below the high peak of French jump racing at Auteuil. There the Grand Steeplechase de Paris (in which Cheltenham Gold Cup winner Captain Christy was second in June 1975) is a race of the mind-boggling value of £48,000 ($82,080)—about the same as Britain's first colts' classic the 2000 Guineas!

At the other end of the French scale, quite unheard of by outsiders, are the little meetings set in the depths of the countryside. Few foreigners will credit it, but there were jumping races on no less than 151 different French provincial tracks in the last six months of 1976.

South-west France is, after Normandy, the second most important horse-breeding area in the state. Their breeders are, like the Irish, mainly farmers keeping two or three mares but Motrico, winner of two Arc de Triomphes, was bred at Biarritz and high-class Nelcius was bred near Bordeaux. The latter has two racecourses, Toulouse and Pau are the next most important and south-west France alone provides 65 different racecourses —more than those in all the United Kingdom.

Below
The Prix M. Labrouche
Steeplechase at Pau

Of the nine territories into which French racing is divided by its different authorities Normandy is so popular that it ranks as two: Basse-Normandie and Haute-Normandie each with its own range of meetings. Three other official racing regions, Anjou-Maine, Ouest (which includes Nantes) and Nord adjoin.

Little courses in Normandy and Brittany close to the Atlantic and handy for British or American visitors include Avranches, Carentan, Corlay, Chateaubriant, Granville, St Malo and Craon (very important for jumping) as well as Nantes. They are Sunday meetings easily accessible from Jersey. The prize money per day varies between £10,000 ($17,100) and £20,000 ($34,200).

One of the fairy-tale rustic courses is sweetly called La Bergerie and lies close to the French National Stud at Le Pin-au-Haras on the outskirts of Gouffern Forest in Normandy, near Argentan (itself a jump racecourse).

The course at La Bergerie holds but three meetings all summer, is surrounded by immense woods and is approached by a long straight road, like a private drive with vast green verges. On one verge stand, dipping and rising, a line of cross country obstacles with several more turning into the belts of sentinel trees. The 2750 acre estate of the National Stud, called the Haras du Pin (a beautiful chateau built in the 1730s on a stud created by Louis XIV three centuries ago), includes several cross-country courses. Of the Three Day Events held there Britain won the 1975 competition with Diana Thorne riding Kingmaker.

The ambience of La Bergerie has a faint whiff of Tweseldown, in the south-east of England; it has strong military ties—several races are restricted to soldiers—and it is delightfully démodé. But where Tweseldown is breezy, La Bergerie sleeps in a forest trilling with birdsong and awakens on only four days a year.

There is but one small and antique stand, carefully built of pink bricks paled by many summers and only 36 yards long. Further along is an embankment affording a view over the spider's web of tracks. These are unrailed except on one side past the winning-post. They greatly resemble a piece of natural country with trees, banks and ditches filling the void in the forest.

For the 4500-metre steeplechases there are 25 obstacles (several jumped in both directions) and for the steeplechase-cross-country 24. These include banks with obstacles topping them, a triple of in-and-out fences in front of the stand, and many open ditches bearded by whiskery fronds. The routes round the web of one outer circuit, two inner circuits connected both with one another and also with the outer one, further intercepted by one internal straight and then two crossed diagonals, make the *parcours* at Cagnes-sur-Mer seem simple. At Pin-au-Haras the track taken resembles a ball of kitten-tangled knitting, and it cannot necessarily ease matters that several races are restricted to Gentleman riders, or to officers and *sous-officiers* and members of the Joinville Batallion.

These antic sports might suggest prize money of point-to-point levels. Yet on two recent autumn Sundays the prize money totalled a staggering £25,200 ($43,092) for the 12 races. These included £16,000 ($27,360), including breeders' prizes, for the six jumping races. The balance is divided among three flat and three trotting races. Additionally the society puts up transport grants: horses coming from further away than 62 miles collect £24 ($41).

Previous page
A bank at Craon. French 'chasing fences often bear more resemblance to natural cross country obstacles than those in English National Hunt courses.

Opposite
The formidable double bank at the Angers-Rennes road at Craon. Here Val Fabio narrowly misses his fallen jockey M. Pascal Adda in the 1976 Prix Georges du Breil Steeple-Chase-Cross-Country The lower photograph on page 108 shows the scene seconds before.

Travelling horses are put up in a beautiful Hans Andersen stable-yard nestling under the forest's fringe behind the spectators' bank. The ancient yard is guarded by the course-keeper's cottage, from which some fairy-tale character seems likely to pop out at any moment.

Certain races are restricted to *non*-thoroughbreds (horses other than '*pur sang anglais*') and these have to be registered as such. Races for this type of horse, similar to the good Anglo-Irish eventer, are common throughout French racing. Between 4 July and 21 November 1976 for example there were 98 steeplechases and steeplechases-cross-country restricted to non-thoroughbreds. Nominal value was seldom below Frs. 10,000 to Frs. 15,000 (£1800 or $3078). The great Mumm race at Craon is the principal non-thoroughbred prize, worth £7300 ($12,483).

All races carry in good French fashion prizes down to the fourth horse, plus additional breeders' '*primes*' of an additional 10 percent or more on the winning owner's prize. In major races there is also an extra owner's '*prime*'. One of the big 4500-metre 'chases at La Bergerie is thus worth £3400 ($5814) to the owner and breeder. The fourth horse in races sagely restricted to a maximum of 18 runners will leave £335 ($573) the richer. Visitors, even if they fail to back a winner, will go home enriched by the ambience of this lovely little place.

The last of our French provincial tracks, Biarritz, is a very different place, but equally charming. You might imagine from the one-time grandeur of the surf-surrounded city that it could be a sort of French Goodwood. After all, Napoleon III built a palace there (now a hotel) in the shape of the E of Empress Eugénie. The aristos followed and built their summer villas. The costly courtesans, 'the grand horizontals' of *la belle époque*, were not far behind, and in their wake swept King Edward VII and his sporting friends. A legacy of *Le High Life* continues faintly in the town, contrasting sharply with the long-haired, wet-suited beach-boys perched like rooks upon their great malibu surf-boards in the bays.

The same extremes apply on the little racecourse on the city's eastern outskirts. The clientele is catholic: the heroic Duke of Alburquerque from Spain a few miles west, the late Marquis de Portago's sister, the Marquise de Mortalla, the president of the course, the Marquis de Roux from Bordeaux, do not come from quite the same background as the cheerful shirtsleeved tourists sucking ices round the neatly hedged parade ring.

The unsaddling enclosure is simply sand, and almost in the Bay of Biscay. The blowing of the horses after their races is drowned by the hungry grinding of the surf. Even in the little private bar next to the secretary's office behind, the wonderful roar of the ocean penetrates the chat of south-western horse-breeding men.

The Edwardian grandstand was razed to the ground by the Germans to build their Atlantic Wall. Now the concrete defence line against an Allied invasion has been gradually grown over with turf: it makes a natural grandstand to overlook the narrow track of the Hippodrome de la Barre.

The course lies between Bayonne and Biarritz. It is gripped between the pincers of the encroaching surf and the golf courses inland. It is exceedingly pretty. On the far side, opposite the plain post-war concrete stand (in which the nobility have private open

Above

The lake at the Hippodrome de la Barre at Biarritz. M. R. Chaignon on Cotero in the lead during the Steeple-Chase-Cross-Country Prix d'Aguiléra, September 1976

boxes on the balcony) is a low and thickly wooded crest. The further side of the course is thus slightly raised. In the centre is a lake used not only for irrigation, but also as an obstacle in the St-Ch Cross Country.

The course, being under one mile round, is nearly as sharp as a dog-track, with a desperately tight turn at the end where the runners, point-to-point fashion, disembark from their park of horse boxes. Since the cross country course requires participants to make some hairpin turns inside the circuit, hunter-trial handiness is of the essence: horses able to spin upon a sou will save lengths.

They will also be required to gallop through the lake, much as at Badminton, but longer and faster and in a racing group—a splendid sight. Contestants, instead of hanging about or dismounting at the start (races are often running an hour late at the end of an afternoon) plunge their horses merrily into the lake and scramble them out again like children on the beach next door, to practise this unusual hazard.

There are walls to be leapt onto, smaller versions of Dublin's old single bank. Then the line shoots off the circuit away from the stands and up a steeply inclined track through the forest of pines beyond the course. The riders flicker behind the trunks then reappear, slithering off an embankment, and corkscrew over a series of cross country obstacles in the course's centre, before rejoining the track proper for the burst home up the straight.

The five-week Biarritz season starts in mid-August on a course which has been in use for over a century. The programmes embrace a selection of races so motley as to seem deliciously comical to serious racegoers' eyes. No-one holidaying in Biarritz's lovely city between the Pyrenees and the sea wishes to take anything, let alone racing, very seriously.

So it is part of the Alice-in-Wonderland charm of the Hippodrome de la Barre to find one race restricted to pure-bred Arabs only (they run $1\frac{1}{2}$ miles on the flat for a £2000 ($3,420) plate) and the next turning out to be one of the richest two-year-old races in all south-west France—with stakes of £7000 ($11,970).

Yet on the same card we see a $2\frac{3}{4}$-mile steeplechase, with owners and breeders prizes rising from a breeders 'prime' of £420 ($718) for the fourth horse home, to the winner's stake of over £4000 ($6840).

The steeplechase-cross-country was run, jumped and twisted over nearly three miles of land and a slice of splashing lake and pounding and slithering pine forest. Its conditions, and its result, fully reflected the highly *sportif* character of French provincial jump racing.

It was, however, with an eye on *égalité*, liberally rewarded: the stakes were worth a startling £4700 ($8037). The eight contestants too comprised the spirit of *fraternité*: four professional men, three gentlemen-riders and one lady amateuse. The last drew warmly approving glances from the crowd including the dark-eyed Spanish Duke: 'très mignonne', nodded the gallant Duc of Alburquerque following the petite and thrustful amazon's progress.

Understandably bemused by the tortuous deviations of the track, the delectable *cavalière* lost her way, as has many a woman before her, when leading her pursuing men a merry dance.

Two of her closest pursuers were not only full-brothers, the sons of Colonel Fagalde, past President for decades of the local Gentlemen Riders Association. They were also riding full-brother horses, similarly bred, reared and trained by the same proud expert and productive Colonel.

It was a great result, rich in the sporting spirit of jump racing in the lovely countryside of France, when the two pairs of brothers, twelve French legs in all, galloped past the winning post at Biarritz in first and third places.

The Colonel and his sons flushed with triumph under the benevolent September sun, and for an instant the tide of applause drowned the incessant rumble of the surf.

Left
Passing the Grandstand in the
Prix Ingré at Craon

Point-to-point and Team Cross Country in Britain

Michael Clayton

Point-to-point

For sheer gallantry in riding over fences at speed it would be hard to beat the sport of point-to-pointing as it is carried on in Great Britain. There is a substantial element of excellent riders and good horses, but inevitably this completely amateur form of racing sees a high proportion of newcomers. No matter how brilliant your own horse, nor how skilfully you ride him, it is all too easy to be brought down by a duck-hearted brute carrying a rider who can neither steer straight nor sit still.

Yet point-to-pointing continues to be one more of the boom areas in equestrian sports since World War II. The economic crisis of the 1970s has shown few signs of discouraging owners or riders. This may be partly because they have never relied on prize money to finance their personal expenditure.

The Jockey Club, which administers the sport, allowed an eight percent increase in the prize money for open races in 1977, but this only meant adding £10 to a first prize of £40. At current levels of costs in buying and keeping point-to-point horses such a figure is derisory. Yet the Jockey Club firmly defends its tight restriction on point-to-point prize money on the grounds that it is the only way to ensure that the sport remains truly amateur, and this may well be right.

The name 'point-to-point' has the same origins as the name 'steeplechase': as described by John Oaksey elsewhere in this book, the first steeplechases were run across country from one village to the next—literally from point to point, these points being the steeples of the village churches.

It all began as a diversion in the hunting-field itself, and then became established as a separate sport, but retaining its roots in the hunt. Each pack registered with the Masters of Foxhounds Association is entitled to hold one point-to-point a year. The runners must qualify for eligibility to race by appearing in the hunting field with one pack of hounds in the current season a minimum of eight times, receiving a certificate attesting to this from a Master of the hunt concerned. This requirement was obviously originally designed to ensure that point-to-point horses were genuine hunters, but has become virtually a ritual in many cases. Some point-to-pointers are properly hunted for at least the early part of the season, being galloped and jumped in pursuit of hounds.

But in most cases the point-to-pointer is merely 'shown' hounds, tit-tupping about for a while at the back end of the field, or on the roads, and then going home early. Some hunts assist in this farce by charging a separate, lower hunt subscription for point-to-pointers. This may be an easy way of raising cash, but it serves to illustrate even more clearly the modern gulf between the genuine hunter and the point-to-point horse.

The problem occurred mainly because of the vastly changing nature of point-to-point courses. Originally, these were simply selected routes across natural country and you needed a horse which could jump the varied fences of the sort which would be encountered in the hunting-field locally. Jumping skill was more desirable than sheer speed, and the highly changeable nature of the terrain in Britain made it far less likely that a horse could go 'pot hunting' far afield as he would be at a considerable disadvantage compared with local horses. For example, racing over walls and banks is a vastly different proposition from racing over thorn hedges and timber.

The first district point-to-point meeting may well have been that held by the Worcestershire Hunt in 1836, but there are various claims of this sort in the 19th century. In 1913 the Masters of Foxhounds Association set up a committee to regularize hunt races, but it was 1929 before the M.F.H.s officially debarred women from racing against men—a rule which remained inflexible until 1967. The old National Hunt Committee, which ruled steeplechasing, took a hand in approving rules for point-to-pointing in 1934. After the war the sport became increasingly popular, but joint control continued between Masters of Foxhounds and the Jockey Club through the Liaison Committee.

The stewards of the Jockey Club maintain control of the sport by allowing that point-to-point meetings held in accordance with Jockey Club regulations are 'recognized'. But a point-to-point meeting which has not been authorized is 'unrecognized', and any horse which has run at such a meeting is perpetually disqualified from racing under point-to-point regulations or the Rules of Racing.

This remains one of the toughest sanctions which the M.F.H.A. can apply against individual hunts. For any hunt which lost its right to hold a point-to-point would be extremely unpopular with its subscribers, landowners and farmers.

Whilst both the Jockey Club and the M.F.H.A. inevitably get criticism from within the sport, it can hardly be denied that their joint control has been of great benefit in ensuring that well defined racing standards are laid down and observed. Furthermore, point-to-pointing through its connection with the Jockey Club has benefited from a slice of the money put back into racing through the Betting Levy. This has provided money for recent course-building improvements.

The regulation minimum height for a point-to-point fence nowadays is 4ft 3in (1.30m) compared with 4ft 6in (1.40m) on a National Hunt course.

The point-to-point horse may not in the same season race under Jockey Club Rules, but there is an excellent opportunity for the successful point-to-pointer to aim higher. The target is the hunter 'chase, a steeplechase held during a National Hunt meeting, but open only to hunters qualified in the hunting field, and amateur riders. Here, both horses and riders get an opportunity to race over bigger fences in racecourse conditions for larger prize money. The champion hunter 'chase, sponsored by *Horse and Hound* at the end of May, is nowadays worth more than £2000 ($3420).

Opposite
Crossing country in a modern hunting-field can mean jumping iron gates as well as more natural obstacles. Here, the whipper-in of the Oakley Hunt in Bedfordshire pops an iron gate during a day's hunting.

Above
Runners for the Open Race in the parade-ring at the annual point-to-point of the Beaufort Hunt

Opposite
Timber racing at the Rappahannock Point-to-Point at Sperryville, Virginia

Point-to-pointing and hunter 'chasing remain the sphere of most horses running in these races, but they have also proved a wonderful nursery for some exceptional horses who have later gone on to race successfully under Rules against the giants at Cheltenham or Aintree. Certainly they provide a wonderful opportunity for young riders to gain experience.

Opportunities for lady riders were until recently considerably limited. They were restricted until 1976 when ladies were permitted to ride in hunter 'chases and the complete range of point-to-point races was being opened to them, the process of liberalization being completed in 1977.

In their first season in hunter 'chases the best lady riders proved themselves to be the equal of men, despite their lack of experience over the bigger fences, reported the *Horse and Hound* Hunter Chasers and Point-to-Pointers Guide, edited by Geoffrey Sale and Ian

Mackenzie. Altogether, more than 2800 horses took part in hunter races in 1976; there were 186 point-to-point meetings; and hunter 'chases were held at 44 race meetings.

The point-to-point and hunter 'chase season starts at the end of February and continues until the end of May, a short but extremely hectic period. As a pure spectacle a point-to-point does not compare with the heights of 'chasing under Rules, but hunter racing has a wonderful atmosphere and the meetings are often extremely well attended. This is partly because each hunt regards the point-to-point meeting as a regular annual treat, attended by many hunt supporters who do not normally go racing. Traditionally, it is an opportunity for the Masters to give tangible thanks to farmers over whose land the pack has been hunting, and these men usually receive complimentary car park tickets.

Although the fences are so much more standardized nowadays, the courses still vary enormously in settings, gradients and types of going. The courses are usually set around several fields on farmland, if possible below naturally rising land where the spectators stand amid tents and a roped-off saddling 'paddock'.

Opposite
Miss J. Ramsay on Willow Walk taking the last fence before going on to win the Pickup Ladies' Open Race at the Derwent Point-to-Point

Below
The Army has made a big contribution to the growing sport of team cross country in Britain. Royal Artillery team members are here on their way to the finish of the Hickstead Team Cross Country Ride.

The small bookmakers who habitually attend point-to-point meetings are a distinct breed in the betting world. The odds offered are seldom very exciting, but there is a considerable amount of betting activity at point-to-points, and there is often a tented Tote booth as well as the bookmakers.

While training costs in other branches of racing continue to escalate, the point-to-point horse is forbidden to be professionally trained during the current season. Only the owner, the owner's groom, or by special permission the proprietor of the stable from where the horse has been hunted, may train the horse.

All this helps to keep costs down, and although a few wealthy riders may occasionally be seen winging their way from one meeting to another by helicopter on the same afternoon, the real backbone of the sport is the farming community, with farmers' sons and daughters riding and training their own horses with the backing of the whole family. They have learned their first lessons in riding over fences in the natural setting of the hunting-field, and the graduation to hunt racing is a normal part of their sporting lives.

What better extension could there be of the natural art and craft of cross country riding?

Above
Point-to-pointing in Ireland: a meeting held by the Scarteen (Black and Tans) pack which has Thady Ryan as Master and huntsman

Team Cross Country

The answer to this question has been supplied in a different way in recent years by the phenomenal growth of another sport which attracts the support and participation of much the same group of people as already fills the point-to-point scene. Far from competing with point-to-pointing, however, the new sport seems to be filling a genuine gap.

I am referring to the Team Cross Country Rides which were invented by Douglas Bunn at his All England Show Jumping Course at Hickstead, Sussex, as a new diversion at his annual Easter meeting. He devised a contest in which teams of four riders rode a course of cross country fences, one team at a time. Their score was the time of the third team member to get home. This has since been amended to teams of five, with the time of the fourth horse being decisive.

Below
Michael Clayton jumps the timber in the Hickstead Cross Country Ride on his Irish-bred hunter Foxford

This may seem rather complicated, but it was a brilliantly clever idea, for it ensured that the ride did not become simply a race, although speed remained important. Although one member could fall or refuse, or otherwise get lost on the way, it was essential for at least three members to pass the finishing line if a score was to be achieved. Thus team members had to stop and assist their colleagues to re-mount, and catch their loose horses if necessary.

Jumping fences in company is not easy, and teams soon learned that it was safer to jump in single file rather than abreast, if the dangers of horses interfering or baulking were to be avoided.

From the start the Hickstead Cross Country was televised and attracted an enthusiastic audience both on and off the course. Using timber, and imposing thorn hedges with ditches and drops, Douglas Bunn provided a challenge which most race-horses would not relish—nor would their owners—but which was ideal for the top-class hunter, eventer or showjumper which had stamina and speed as well as jumping ability.

The Team Cross Country Ride immediately attracted amazingly wide support with hunting folk, under various titles, providing the hard core. There were representatives from the House of Lords, the House of Commons, the racing, eventing, and showjumping worlds, and the Services responded magnificently. The public loved to see the teams having a go, although the persistence of a few riders in putting a refuser repeatedly at a big fence earned criticism from some quarters, notably those who are ever on the look out for the 'welfare' of horses performing in public.

Above
Army riders take the drop fence, second on the course in the Hickstead Ride

Although such scenes were not especially edifying, they were a very small part of an excellent new amateur sport, and Douglas Bunn insisted on continuing with the bare minimum of rules. He asserted that the size of the fences, and the challenge of riding them, would in time ensure that unsuitable horses were not entered, and the sport would find its own level of competition.

His first Ride was in 1974 and immediately it spawned a host of imitators up and down Britain, mainly run by hunts on Sunday afternoons, as an enjoyable treat and as a new means of raising money.

The early participation of Princess Anne and Capt. Mark Phillips ensured the interest of the wider public, and it was not long before commercial sponsorship was readily available.

Yet because the sport lacked overall administration and rules, the courses already varied widely. Some, such as the Zetland Hunt's Ride, in Yorkshire, had beautifully made imposing fences which required skilful riding, yet there were easier alternative fences which took longer to reach and thus ensured that time was its own penalty for those choosing them. This meant that moderate or novice horses could still get round the courses and provide immense fun and experience for their riders, while the way was also clear for the better combinations to win by boldly jumping the bigger fences.

The Zetland course, for example, included a 5ft 2in (1.60m) wall on a slight downhill gradient, and some hedges with formidable drops on the landing side, but the easy alternatives to these were straightforward timber 'tiger trap' fences.

Yet some other courses were proving far too easy all the way round, encouraging teams to gallop flat-out and hurdle their fences, a particularly dangerous practice across country. Some competitors, notably the Zetland Farmers' team, complained publicly

Below
Ladies traditionally hunted side-saddle in the past, and some do so today. Here Mrs Sarah Sherwin and her sister Mrs Annabel Holt ride side-saddle in a recent Yorkshire Team Cross Country event

The end of the race for a hopeful amateur participating in an English point-to-point

about this and warned organizers to provide better-built fences to avoid the dangers of undue speed and to provide a better spectacle.

At the beginning of 1977 the British Horse Society was arranging a meeting of all interested parties, and it was possible that some form of agreed rules would be drawn up; but some folk insisted that this would be a retrograde step, and the progress of the sport in the next few years is still somewhat in doubt.

A rather different sort of Team Cross Country Ride remains the Melton Hunt Club's annual Ride in Leicestershire, which is the closest link with the old point-to-point in its original form.

Up to 70 riders assemble in a field, and are flagged away to ride over natural Leicestershire country to a finishing line some four miles away. It is up to each rider to take the shortest route his skill and courage will allow, and inevitably the challenge takes its toll at some of the fences.

The Quorn, Belvoir and Cottesmore alternate as hosts to the Ride, and afterwards the hunt concerned brings its hounds to the scene and a day's hunting follows in the area.

In 1975 I rode in the Melton Ride held in the Belvoir Wednesday country. It was tremendous fun, with the line of the Ride crossing the Melton Brook. It was a wet season, with deep going, and only 54 of us finished, out of 70 starters.

Afterwards, on a fresh horse, I followed the Belvoir hounds in a remarkable 15-mile run from the famous Melton Spinney covert.

The Ride had been fun, but the hunt was far more exciting, because the pleasure of riding to hounds is far richer: the uncertainties of scent, the fox's wiles, and the natural hazards of the countryside, make the route a constant adventure, and the thrill of hearing hounds cry and watching them stream ahead over natural country is unique.

Cross Country Rides on a competitive basis will no doubt flourish and proliferate, but their roots are still as strong as ever—in the hunting-field.

Below
Catherine Wills on Rabicano, in The Eventers Ladies Team at Hickstead, 1974

From Grand National to Badminton

Chris Collins

There are two sides to steeplechasing. There are the thrills and the victories; there are also the falls and the injuries, the narrow defeats and the sadnesses which befall the horses. After I started point-to-pointing in 1958, I spent years in the wilderness experiencing mostly the bad and at least once was on the point of giving up.

Then came the great good fortune of a third in the 1965 Grand National on Mr Jones. This provided the encouragement I needed and I kicked on to become Leading Amateur for a couple of seasons. However, this era of my riding ended with a crashing fall at Hexham in May 1968, the sale of most of my horses and getting down to work again. I hunter-'chased the following spring on the few horses I had kept, but it was clear that I was not the jockey I had been when doing it full time. With the end of my racing apparently in sight, should I perhaps take up another branch of riding to take over from it? In fact, I thought of either eventing or showjumping. I discussed my problem with Johnny Kidd, who was then jumping more or less full-time. He strongly advised eventing as showjumping was too professional for me to have any hope of getting anywhere. He also suggested I went to Lars Sederholm, whose establishment was near and who was a top trainer of event riders and horses.

I accepted this advice without reservation and made an appointment to see Lars, with whose clear, matter-of-fact thinking I was immediately impressed. I also reasoned that he must be good as Richard Walker, who was his product, had won the 1969 Badminton. We discussed my ideas and at the end of a short conversation I asked him to start looking for horses, which he would train and on which I would have lessons. The first target was Badminton the following spring. I was not expecting this to be very successful (and it wasn't) but I thought it sensible to throw myself in the deep end and start building up big match experience as soon as possible.

Interestingly, at the outset I completely underestimated the difficulties of eventing. In retrospect I was influenced by my steeplechasing experience of being Leading Amateur within one year of setting my mind to it. I failed to take into account all the time I had spent blundering about picking up some ideas about the game and learning by mistakes.

For at least two years I hardly got anywhere. I found the dressage difficult. Being so used to riding short, ridiculous as it sounds, it was hard for me to keep my feet in the stirrups. One foot bounced out once in the middle of a test in Switzerland and at Burghley one year I resorted to tying them in with black thread. I also made stupid mistakes through being overbold and rash in the cross country. For a long time I regarded it as *de rigueur* to jump all fences the most difficult way. This was the 'kick on regardless' legacy from steeplechasing.

In fact, as I eventually learned, it is necessary to have a quite different attitude towards eventing—more that of the surgeon, calmly doing a job with precision. A balance must be struck between speed and safety, as the delivery of a clear round is essential. In fact it is no bad rule, at a Three Day Event, to jump every fence the easiest way. The skill is to produce a fast round without taking undue risks. Risks will obviously pay off sometimes, but will inevitably lead to falls and refusals if taken repeatedly. It is essential to keep cool in the dressage and showjumping. Losing one's relaxation has a snowball effect. One sees (and has ridden) tests which start off well, then something goes wrong, and the whole performance disintegrates completely.

In 'chasing, if you fail to win one day there is nearly always another chance quite soon, even at the highest level. If a horse gets unluckily beaten in the Cheltenham Gold Cup, there is still the Whitbread and other big races for him later that season. It is therefore sensible for a jockey to have a do-or-die cut at the last and risk falling in order to win, particularly as second place means nothing. Eventing at the top level is more a question of building up consistency. Also, Badminton dominates the British eventing calendar to a far greater extent than even the Derby does flat racing. Not only is it the British Championship, but on form shown at it the selectors base the team for the international championship later in the year. It is therefore essential to deliver at Badminton.

Every year I have driven away from Badminton after something has gone wrong. I have blown the dressage, or had a silly refusal in the cross country, or dropped several places by knocking down a show-jump when marks were close. Every time I have realized that there was further work to be done, that the base to my riding was not strong enough when it came to the crunch of the big time.

Although my eventing brought no results for some time, by inspiring me to put more into the actual riding of the horses it did provide a 'shot-in-the-arm' for my racing. At the end of the spring of 1969 I had felt that my racing prospects were pretty gloomy and that soon I would have to start riding made horses only on my way out.

Fortunately I did buy one more young horse. I combined my cousin's wedding one June Saturday with a call on W.A. Stephenson to see a five-year-old that he said was my type. Kit Stobbs and I were sent out to see him. We caught up a big, lazy, brown horse and clapped a saddle and bridle on him. Kit legged me up and I cantered up the field and back. We went back and WA asked me what I thought. 'Very nice type, his movement a little high, but that might have been because of the long grass. Could possibly have had a little more bone.' WA's reply was 'Nor, Nor' to the question of bone and that he could guarantee the movement. I said right, I was interested. He named the price and as usual we dealt without bargaining. The horse, unlike most of my purchases from WA, had a name, which was Credit Call. He came down to Leicestershire for me to hunt that winter and all the time I had an increasing feeling that he was a good horse. He radiated class, and indeed he proved it with a vengeance, carrying me to win about 25 races over the next five years.

Opposite
Chris Collins on Smokey taking the Taxis fence at Badminton. The fence was named in his honour after the fence of the same name at Pardubice which was associated with his triumph there.

With Credit Call winning six races in 1970 and Ballino four, my racing had
something of a revival, and by the end of the season I had adopted the policy which was
to serve me for the rest of my racing career. By now I was beginning to get a feel of what
I liked in the way of horses—a 16.2 strong enough for me to imagine myself out
hunting on, but with quality, good Irish back-breeding, good movement and preferably
bay or brown (a chestnut had to be that much nearer to perfection for me to buy). This
was a type WA liked as well and he would buy them whenever he saw them in Ireland;
he would get them over young and would break them, usually at the age of four, in the
quiet period between jumping seasons. Every year I would go up at this time and would
buy two or three.

They would stay there until November, learning to gallop and perhaps getting as
far as a school over hurdles round a racecourse. They would then go down to be schooled
on the flat and taught to jump by Lars and his lieutenants as if they were young
competition horses. Meanwhile, by 1 January my other horses would have gone back
into training so the young ones came to take their places in Noel Pegge's high-class
Leicestershire yard. Later in the year they would either have the odd point-to-point or
would go back to the North for a couple of runs over hurdles. Racing-wise nothing
much was expected—my main aim was to get some experience into them. They would
then come down to Leicestershire the following autumn in time for the opening meet
and become regular hunter-'chasers in the spring. This long preparation for the real
thing gave these powerful young horses time to develop and I got a great kick out of
hunting them properly.

The year 1971, except for my riding my hundredth winner on Credit Call, was
disappointing. At the dinner tables of Leicestershire after the port had circulated several
times, there was the occasional suggestion that eventing was having a bad effect on my
riding and that I was past it. Whether or not because of this, matters improved in 1972.
Credit Call went through the hunter-'chase season unbeaten, winning the Cheltenham
and Liverpool Foxhunters, and the *Horse and Hound* Cup. I also managed to win the
Melton Cross Country race by a short head on my hunter Quiz.

Furthermore, I was beginning to make progress on the eventing front. I managed to
win my first One Day Event and Centurian, apart from one hiccup, went a great gallop
round Badminton to finish twelfth. Unfortunately, I had disregarded Lars' advice to go
the easy way at the Munich pen. Centurian had gone fast and brilliantly and I
confidently attempted the corner. Between us we misjudged the line. I found myself
into the pen, out over some palings on the far side and right over the wire fence set
round the jump to keep spectators back. At this point I fell off but as we were outside
the penalty zone only the refusal counted. However, I was faced with the problem of
getting back onto the course and carrying on. The fence Judge offered to lay his tweed
coat on the wire so I could jump back in. This I declined, so he lowered the wire and
eventually I was on my way again.

This was a classic example of the over-bold approach which does not yield results in
eventing. Later in the day I watched Mark Phillips and Richard Meade, first and second
that year, going up the chute, which took time but converted the pen into an easy fence.
The next day, between the veterinary inspection and the showjumping, Lars held a *post
mortem* with myself and Richard Walker who had also got into trouble. I at last began to

Below
Credit Call, on which Chris
Collins has ridden more than
100 wins, in the 1972 *Horse
and Hound* Cup at
Stratford-upon-Avon

realize that in eventing one has to play safe.

I had greatly appreciated my rides at the Three Day Events at Frauenfeld, Switzerland, in 1970, and Boekelo, Holland, in 1971. So when a group of Swedish sportsmen invited Bill Shand Kydd and myself over for their Grand National in May 1972, I was pleased enough to accept. I selected Hilbirio for the job. He was a lovely type of horse, then only six. In his early races I had had what I described as difficulty in achieving a real rapport and what WA described as 'not being able to ride one side of

him', but things were improving. He was a bold horse out hunting, with a terrific jump, and would certainly have the courage to tackle strange fences.

The horses flew out with Bill's trainer Bryan Thompson in an old, hippo-like former freighter, and we followed by conventional airline in time for a school the day before the race. In fact very few of the fences were small enough for us to tackle and when we did get going we nearly mowed down a group of children who were courageously holding a sack-race just round a rather sharp bend. Try as I would I could not get Hilbirio to jump *through* the rather soft fences. He insisted on clearing them with brilliant leaps which I feared would take too much out of him in the race.

It poured with rain and none of the English contingent, except possibly the fearless Biddlecombe who was riding for Norway, were sorry to hear the whine of power saw when we got to the course to walk round on the morning of the race. The biggest jump, over six feet in height but brushable through, was being cut down. I missed out on the pre-race cocktail party to spend more time sauna-ing—as usual the weight was a problem. The small changing-room, whose roof did duty as the grandstand, was shared with several attractive ladies due to ride in an earlier race. Unlike Bill, I was too weak from my wasting and general apprehension to appreciate their Nordic charms properly.

In the race Hilbirio rose to the occasion. He jumped brilliantly and without thwarting him I could not prevent him hitting the front a mile out. Round the last bend he died a bit in the heavy ground and it seemed endless—finally he just held on to beat Barry Brogan on a Polish-bred Norwegian horse.

I was thrilled and in the aftermath decided that I would ride in as many Three Day Events and races abroad as possible. I was lucky enough to be second in the Norwegian National and win the Swedish National again in 1973 with Hilbirio. Credit Call won the first hunter 'chase in Ireland open to English horses in 1974. I rode in the South African Whitbread Horse Trials in 1974 and in the Meikles Trials in Rhodesia in 1975 on borrowed horses, as well as taking my own horses to America, Holland, Ireland and Switzerland. Undoubtedly, however, what I appreciated the most were my experiences in Czechoslovakia in connection with the Grand Pardubice Steeplechase.

I had known of this historic race for some time, as John Oaksey had referred to it when the Russian horses came over for the British Grand National in the early sixties. Gradually it came to the forefront of my consciousness and after my experiences in Scandinavia it appeared to be the logical next step.

In June 1973 I flew out to Prague to inspect the course, to put into perspective the more fearsome descriptions of it, and to decide which horse to take. I was whisked out to Pardubice in a black government car with Babanek, the Director General of Racing, and an interpreter, and spent the day trudging round the course under a broiling sun which later gave way to sticky rain.

I was genuinely horrified by the Taxis fence—a straight-up, 5ft (1.50m) high and 5ft thick fence with a 16ft 6in (5m) ditch on landing. To begin with I thought I had been shown it as a joke and that it was in fact a sort of giant boundary between different sections of the course. After being assured that horses did clear it, I saw that it was jumpable at racing pace if everything went right. I didn't much like the big waters, and the amount of waving corn which by October would give way to plough would ensure

that the whole affair would be a gigantic test of stamina. Having got so far I decided that I had better have a go and that Stephen's Society was the horse for the job. He was a seven-year-old, great quality bulldozer who so far had failed to win a race, but was a brilliant hunter.

Not much went right with his preparation. He came in from the field coughing and then got beaten in his two preparatory runs, blowing heavily after both. It took from dawn on the Monday until 10pm on the Wednesday for him to reach Pardubice, stopping overnight at pre-arranged places under the care of Charlie, my driver, and Sue, who normally looked after my event horses. His appearance excited great interest when I took him out onto the course for a few practice jumps on the Friday morning. Unfortunately he rather dented our image by promptly refusing at a small island bank in the middle of a field. He was a little difficult at Fence 3, a small water, which I took him over backwards and forwards several times, but jumped some hedges extremely well. Afterwards the consensus was that he was lacking in elegance for a racehorse, his arrival three days before the race in contrast to the Russians' three weeks was casual, and that my three-pound saddle was ridiculous for the Pardubice.

I spent that afternoon walking the course, charting where the plough was lightest and evaluating the best places to take the fences. That evening we attended a veterinary lecture, which, as it was delivered in Czech, was of limited benefit to me. However, it was followed by some films of previous Pardubices which were of real value. Up to then

I had rather fancied the idea of jumping Taxis, the fourth fence, in front on the left where it was lowest. In order to avoid the risk of getting brought down one would have to get there first, but they seemed to go off at such a pace that it looked as if this would not be possible for Stephen. I therefore decided I must have an alternative. Plan A would be to jump off in front. Plan B would be to let them go, and jump the big part of Taxis on the right, where I would be more likely to get a free passage.

The next morning I gave Stephen a good gallop and jumped some more fences. He blew but there was nothing more to be done. The rest of the morning was occupied by the jockeys' briefing, again in Czech, which meant rather less to me than the others. In the afternoon I walked the course again meticulously. At 7pm sharp the Chefs d'Équipe's dinner took place. As the sole British representative I was invited. The hierarchy started with the Russian trainer on the right of Babanek and worked its way down via West Germans, Bulgars and Czechs to myself at the bottom of the table. I pecked as sparingly as possible at the fare. I was worried about my weight.

The next day at the course there was a festive atmosphere. Streamers streamed, trumpets blared, whistles blew and there were many thousands of people. I was worried about Stephen's fitness, Taxis and the opposition and could not see us doing well. The trip was a reconnaissance and afterwards I would know if it was worth returning another year to try to win.

Below
An early win for Chris Collins in the *Horse and Hound* Cup at Stratford-upon-Avon, 1966, on Santa Grand

Above
Chris Collins (in the quartered cap) remounting after a fall at the 'Great Waterlogged Ditch' in the Pardubice Steeplechase in Czechoslovakia in 1974

Finally the preliminaries were disposed of and we were away in the race. The early pace was terrific and far too much for Stephen. I adopted Plan B. As we swung into Taxis most of the field made left for the easier end of it. I kept Stephen hard right and gave him a real shake-up 50 yards away. He went on towards the fence and took off close to it, not throwing much of a leap. 'Christ, we're going in the ditch!' I thought and leaned so far back I practically touched his quarters with the back of my head. In fact he touched lightly down, weaved his way through the odd faller and made nothing of the Irish bank and the next two fences. Then came a hiccup. At the In and Out we were carried out by a loose horse. I rejoined the race at least 50 lengths to the bad. Incredibly, without me hurrying him, after another mile and a half or so Stephen had made this up. We got over the waters, a horse fell at the next and we were third with a mile-and-a-half to go. We bided our time and let a Czech horse kick on. We survived the remaining difficult fences and came on to the racecourse for the last time, second and full of running. At the second last we jumped past the leader, galloped into the straight in front, cleared the last, a simple hurdle, and held on to win by eight lengths.

There was a great ceremonial to winning. Six-foot rosettes were presented, the Union Jack hoisted, God Save the Queen played and we jockeys presented to the high officials. Later Stephen was asked to print his foot onto a racecard to give his autograph and I to make over my colours to the hippological museum.

I went back the following year to find lots of friends, but also a certain feeling that as it was the hundredth anniversary of the race a Czech should win. Reports of threats to ride me off the course kept reaching me. Whatever their substance—there was a lot of early jostling and one of the Russians did his best to chop me in half at Fence 2—they certainly had an unnerving effect. It was partially because I took exaggerated care to get a clear passage at Taxis that we fell. Fortunately although I was thrown clear it took

Stephen as long as me to get to his feet, so I was able to catch him and clamber on, rather ingloriously, my attempt to vault on failing as he cantered off, forcing me to put my foot in the stirrup. We caught up after two miles only to part company again at the second water. I misjudged the approach, Stephen put in a short one and dropped his hind legs into the river. I remounted and we finally finished third. Although it was disappointing not to win again, I did feel that we had tried and that our falls did in a way embody the spirit of the Pardubice. The Russians rode under strict orders to remount and finish at all costs. At least, as the sole representative of the decadent West, I had managed not to throw in the sponge.

During these years I had climbed a few rungs up the eventing ladder. In the autumn of 1973 Centurian was placed at Burghley, in England, and Ledyard Farm, USA. I had the great good fortune to buy Smokey VI from Bill Powell-Harris, a dashing Irish cross country rider, and managed to finish third on him in Holland. The following spring I came ninth and tenth on those two horses at Badminton, which resulted in my being asked to join the short-list for the World Championships. They were held at Burghley and after a good summer Smokey and I finally made the team. Unfortunately, things went wrong and we had two falls, partly because I went too fast and partly because he wasn't right in himself on cross country day.

By 1975 I had begun to think of turning totally to eventing. My mind was finally made up by a fall at the Cheltenham hunter-'chase meeting in which I crushed four vertebrae. It was becoming increasingly clear that if I was to get anywhere in eventing I should now buckle down to it as seriously as possible. The hours spent steaming off excess weight and dashing up to the northern racetracks could be profitably re-allocated to dressage competitions, showjumping and generally working away at my riding. The old days of riding in a hunter-'chase at Perth one day and then tackling the Badminton dressage the next were magnificent but not what won a Three Day Event. The decision having been taken, to my great surprise I found myself in no way missing the racing, by which I had been enslaved for nearly twenty years. Instead as I got deeper into eventing I have found myself more and more fascinated by the game and attracted by its different challenges.

Left
Chris Collins on Centurian coming off the Normandy Bank at Badminton

EVENTING

Horse trials, eventing or combined training is the youngest branch of formalized cross country riding. It had its origins in the Army cavalry schools of continental Europe.

The second day of a Three Day Event is the Speed and Endurance test, of which the cross country phase is the most important element in the whole competition. (The first day is devoted to Dressage and the third to Showjumping, both of which contribute relatively much less to the overall result. The Speed and Endurance test includes roads and tracks and a steeplechase as well as the cross country course.)

The Three Day Event first appeared in the Olympic Games in 1912, when the Swedes were the gold medallists. It remains a firmly-established international sport with a regular programme from the Olympics to the European and World Championships.

In the past decade eventing has seen considerable growth in Europe and the United States. The participation of Princess Anne in the 1976 Olympics in Canada emphasized the strong royal interest in the sport in Britain. Princess Anne was European champion at Burghley in 1971, but the United States won the team and individual gold medals at the 1976 Olympics.

One Day and Two Day Events proliferate and offer experience at novice and intermediate levels, but the Three Day Event remains the ultimate test, with Britain's Badminton, America's Ledyard Farm and Germany's Luhmühlen among the most daunting courses in the world.

Eventing in Great Britain

Ann Martin

Since John Shedden won the inaugural Badminton Horse Trials on Golden Willow in 1949 from a field of 22, British interest in Three Day Events has grown continuously. In 1976 there were 109 entries for Badminton: 70 horses started. The mere handful of One Day Events that took place in the early fifties has grown into two official, highly packed seasons, one in spring and one in autumn.

In 1977, under the aegis of the Combined Training Group, a highly organized section of the British Horse Society, some 80 One, Two and Three Day Events were held. The vast majority were sponsored by the Midland Bank, whose continuing interest in horse trials at all levels has considerably helped their rapid development.

The Combined Training Group reported record registration numbers in November 1976: 3406 horses and 3392 members. Even with 80 horse trials well spaced throughout the length and breadth of the country, from the initial foray at Penzance in Cornwall in mid-March, through fixtures in Kent, East Anglia, Wales and Scotland, to the season's close at the Duke of Devonshire's beautiful Chatsworth House in Derbyshire, would-be competitors are often frustrated because trials are over-subscribed and entries are returned.

This growth reflects not only the fact that the horse is extremely popular as a means of relaxation and escape from the stresses and strains of life in the late 20th century, but also the enormous challenge and excitement of riding across country.

Great Britain has a good record in eventing, having been virtually unbeatable from 1967 to 1972, winning both the Mexico and the Munich Olympic gold team medals and the 1970 World Championship. The surge of popularity of the sport in the United States, combined with the US acquisition of the brilliant French trainer Jack Le Goff, meant that in 1974 the world title crossed the Atlantic westwards, as did the Olympic gold in 1976.

The hunting-field plays an important contributory role in Britain's success, by instilling in a competition horse the urge to go forward—making him want to jump the diverse range of obstacles, among them hedges, ditches, gates, cattle-troughs, post-and-rails, streams and banks. Horses are gregarious and their natural herd instinct tends to make them enthusiastic about following other horses during the hunt.

Such experiences as crossing water in the hunting-field are also useful for the novice eventer. In competition, cross country riding is totally different and although the horse starts with one or two inviting fences, he soon faces some surprises which must be overcome regardless, with only his education and rider's encouragement upon which to rely.

Part of the fascination of eventing is that success demands the complete horse, sufficiently supple and obedient to complete the dressage test, bold and courageous across a range of solid and demanding cross country fences, and then after these exertions still able to complete a small but twisty show jumping course with control and accuracy.

Across country a horse must develop an enquiring mind to see, accept and take on any hazards he may encounter on uneven or sloping terrain, including ditches, coffins, quarries, and bounce fences. He must also enter water without hesitation and learn that when he approaches at a freer pace, he jumps over, not into the water.

In three day eventing it is essential to analyse what effect the steeplechase will have on the cross country phase, as no matter what the course is like, it will have some latent bearing. If the steeplechase is run on top of the ground and the horse goes very freely and easily, a horse that is not used to steeplechase fences could be brought down because he is running away with himself and his own balance. If the steeplechase phase contains much undulation, this could knock a horse out of rhythm. All these factors could be tiring and put the horse a shade wrong into the fences of the cross country phase. If the horse is tired after the steeplechase, the rider needs to take a firm hold initially to give his horse a secure start, at a different slower pace, and work up the pace gradually. Two riders with the experience and first class judgement of pace who regularly achieve this are Olympic gold team medallists Richard Meade and Jane Holderness-Roddam.

Another Olympic gold medallist Laurie Morgan has said, 'I start the steeplechase course fast, then I am able to allow my horse a let up so I can come again.' Kicking on a tired horse at the start of the cross country is a sure way of failing to make the trip but you need all the experience of this great Australian to carry out his plan with success.

Many experts regard Badminton Horse Trials as the world's greatest Three Day Event. Certainly it is the one that the British riders seek to win above all others. The famous course, basically the same each year, is set in the superb park of the Duke of Beaufort's Badminton House near Bath. The excellent old turf provides fast going, contributing to thrilling competition. Throughout the season, and more particularly in the spring, certain one day horse trials are favoured by riders as work-outs for their Badminton horses.

Brigstock Horse Trials in March are much favoured as an easy Badminton school. They are run by the redoubtable Diana Maxwell, who has an endless capacity for work and the necessary brand of cheerfulness, in the grounds of her family home, Fermyns Wood Hall, near Kettering, in Northamptonshire. Horses cannot have too much schooling over ditches and there are many examples of this hazard here.

In late March, Downlands in Hampshire provides a course where the jumps look deceptively small and fairly simple as you walk round before the competition; in fact, there are always many stops and falls. There is a tremendous variety of obstacles, including a difficult water-jump and a combination of banks and post-and-rails with a

Previous page
Combinations are not frequently met in cross country riding, but they do occur in eventing courses. Here the horse has 'gone on' too strongly at the first part—and paid the penalty at the second element.

Opposite
Princess Anne and Goodwill—the horse she rode in the Bromont Olympics in 1976—touching down off the Normandy Bank at Badminton

bounce having an effect similar to a coffin. Varied terrain makes it a tiring course.

It was a real loss when David Engleheart's Kinlet Horse Trials held near Bewdley, Shropshire, usually in late March, were not included in the 1977 fixture list, due to a clash of dates with the local point-to-point. These are real top-of-the-world trials, centred on a hill in front of elegant Kinlet Hall in the Wyre Forest. The visibility over the surrounding country from the extremely well built and imaginative course could scarcely be bettered. Such jumps as the Water Garden, a water complex, are not just masterpieces of design and construction generously decorated with primroses and polyanthus, but also very testing. No less a person than former European Champion Sheila Willcox suffered a reversal there but returned the following year with typical determination to set matters right. This sophisticated event is specially favoured by many riders, among them internationals Chris Collins and Janet Hodgson, because of the quality of the fences and the steep hills which provide a really searching pre-Badminton blow-out. The horses really have to use their lungs, their riders finding out exactly how fit or unfit they really are. Although set high on a hill, the undulating show-jumping arena is apt to become holding in wet weather.

Set in Wiltshire in the vale of Pewsey between the Marlborough downs and Salisbury Plain, Rushall, which is also held in late March, is another good pre-Badminton outing. There are opportunities to jump into water, and while not particularly tiring, there are a few formidable fences that really open up a horse.

In the north, Corbridge and Fenton provide two true galloping courses in late March and early April. The former is sited north-east of Corbridge adjacent to Hadrian's Wall. Full use has been made of the quarries used by the Romans when building the wall nearly 2000 years ago. There are few island obstacles; the fences are solid and well constructed—none of the flimsy handiwork seen at certain trials—and some solid walls. Most riders who have competed there single out the Vallum, the ditch running on the south side of the wall, which has been incorporated into a unique obstacle with a very steep descent.

The long established Fenton, owned by Lord Lambton, lies near Wooler between Edinburgh and Newcastle and enjoys fine views of the Cheviot hills. Most efficiently organized by Lord and Lady Joicey, it features a wide variety of fences with plenty of timber.

And so we come to Badminton, one of the high-points of the season. Badminton has two great assets. The land lends itself exceptionally well to a Three Day Event, while former international Colonel Frank Weldon is an extremely talented course-builder. He asks a series of big questions, and for hesitant, reluctant or critical riders, there is always the disconcerting and restricting thought that this former European Champion and Badminton winner might leap onto the nearest horse at the drop of a hat and make a nonsense of their worries. Colonel Weldon is sufficiently bold to try something new if he considers it will improve horse and rider and has the intelligence and courage to change it the following year, if, in his opinion, it does not prove totally successful. One can always be certain that horses will be fully tested because the Badminton Speed, Cross Country and Endurance Day makes great demands of the horses' condition and riders' horsemastership. The steeplechase course is a tough assignment for the horse because at the end of the track there is a small amount of ridge and furrow, so the horses start the cross country having done a fair bit of work beforehand.

Above

Triple gold medallist Richard Meade, riding the comparatively inexperienced Jacob Jones, jumped clear round the Olympic Three Day Event cross country course at Bromont. Here they are coming over the third element at the lake.

From a psychological point of view, because it has been run for so long and has been a severe test for many years, Badminton commands great respect from riders who arrive both excited and nervous rather like jockeys immediately before the Grand National.

The Duke of Beaufort founded Badminton in 1949. The previous year he had been to Aldershot to watch the Olympic Three Day Event. It was the first ever to be held in England and was regarded by many British hunting and point-to-point enthusiasts with distrust. Earlier participation in Olympic equestrian events had been confined to the Army. The British team did not finish in 1948 because a horse became lame, but the Duke was impressed by the way the competition seemed suited to the various characteristics and attributes of the British horse. The British event world is permanently indebted to him for subsequently offering his magnificent Gloucestershire estate for a similar competition each year.

Opposite
Diana Thorne and The
Kingmaker jumping the
trakehner at Cirencester. The
Kingmaker was runner-up in
the 1977 Badminton Trials.

Badminton results matter for the top riders because the selectors are always present to make up the shortlist for the year's major international competition. It is springtime, the leaves are budding, the grass is getting greener; it is a time of anticipation and even with the occasional below-average entry, Badminton never fails to produce an enthralling contest.

One absorbing feature of the cross country course is that some old favourites such as the Luckington Lane crossings and Tom Smith's Walls appear regularly alongside new tests. Usually, the course, which may be run clockwise or anti-clockwise, starts with a couple of easy fences, such as the Timber Stack and Woodpile in 1976, to help the horse adjust, but soon a fence such as Huntsman's Close may loom ahead. This is difficult not only because it is a formidable obstacle, but because the horse encounters darker surroundings and many trees. There may well be a drop fence in the centre which can come as a shock to the horse, and then immediately a rather sharp turn which is a big test on uneven going before the horse has re-settled and established his rhythm.

After the first Luckington Lane crossing, jumps onto and off the road with stiff drops that set the horses back a little, the horse may have to be bold over a ditch. Then he may face the Cat's Cradle where either the middle can be taken with courage, or a totally different problem mastered by jumping the two wings at a chosen angle. The Quarry is seldom really formidable, but the horse must show real respect because the drop is considerable and shortly afterwards he may have to bring all his power into play to negotiate two banks. After such an exertion, he must have a chance to recover and regain his wind. Then, even should he meet one of the biggest obstacles such as the Faggot Pile, there are no major problems.

The Trakehner, over a ditch, presents a test of courage where the horse must clear a big heavy pole with a lot of air underneath. On one famous occasion Rachel Bayliss's Gurgle the Greek elected to negotiate it by scrambling beneath.

An apparently pleasant fence such as the Park Wall may follow but, with a sloping take-off, the ground line can be misleading. If, about half way round, the horse is tiring after several unexpected experiences, the Vicarage Ditch would seem difficult. The fact that this caused more trouble in early days than in the 1970s is perhaps attributable to the angle of the approach. If the horse can see it well out, he has ample time to look into it, hesitate and refuse, or perhaps sustain a mental set-back through endeavouring to bank it: whereas, if it is more flat, the horse can be shaken up, galloped in and over, all before he realizes.

Tom Smith's Walls, set at right-angles to each other, are extremely solid and very unforgiving. Few people attempt the corner because as a rule it does not pay off, but nevertheless, the obstacle presents a sharp angle, and the decision remains whether to approach at an angle or fit in a larger loop, which of course wastes time.

If jumped slightly upwards, the second Luckington Lane crossing consists of a formidable hedge. It is therefore hard for the horse to gain ground on the stride between the fences, which is fairly long, and again immense courage and spirit are needed. Should the horse be tired, he could be casual at the later Open Water, and end up with a tumble.

After a few more simple fences, the horse approaches the Coffin. He will already have encountered both big and problem fences and now he will meet the type of obstacle that causes more problems than any other. At this stage of the game, the horse does not draw in and pop through easily—he has seen so much and had so many surprises that if the rider does not take every precaution possible by instilling respect in him with a short, sensible, onward-bound stride, a stop may be the result. If the rider is also tired, he can easily pay the penalty and fall off because this type of jump often causes the horse to hit either himself or the jump, thus unseating his rider.

Finally, there is usually a long gallop towards home, although even at this stage there remains the hazard of the Lake. Too wide a jump into the Lake at Badminton necessitates no less than a swim, an indignity suffered by Olympic riders as well as the less experienced. Captain Mark Phillips, for example, suffered an immersion on Brazil in 1976. The huge crowd at the Lake adds to the stress. As Swedish trainer Lars Sederholm once commented when walking the course with Jan Jonssen, the Swedish Champion, and international Chris Collins, 'If you fall off here you'll be doing it in a big way. Many have fallen off at the Trout Hatchery at Burghley,' he continued, 'but there they seldom do worse than get their breeches wet.'

There are few Welsh Trials but Llanfechain at Bodynfoel Halls, in Powys just within the Welsh border, provides a scenic setting with some mountainous ascents and descents. Many jumps are placed round the Afon Cain which flows along the course. These Trials are unusual, featuring both Novice and Intermediate Two Day Events.

Without doubt, Tidworth is the simplest and best Three Day Event for young novice combinations. It is staged in the park of Tidworth House, the Officers Club at the Wiltshire Army Garrison Town. Unfortunately, the comparatively recent steeplechase course is tiring and uninteresting, but the cross country course run on the top of the ground plays a valuable part on the circuit because horses find it easier than most Three Day Events. On the other hand, for spectators, the cross country course, rather strangely, lacks atmosphere; but the final day's showjumping offers a pleasant sense of occasion.

In early June, many riders with up-and-coming horses make the trip to West Yorkshire where George Lane Fox directs the Bramham Three Day Event mainly in the park surrounding his fine colonnaded Queen Anne house. This lush, verdant setting in well wooded land is incorporated into the cross country section. The steeplechase fences are outstanding, but the course sometimes proves a little strenuous for a young horse that is not properly fit.

The highlight of the autumn season, which opens in late July or early August, is the Burghley Three Day Event in early September. This often has an international ambience and the time of year and the facilities, together with the backcloth of the imposing, extravagantly turreted, Elizabethan Burghley House at Stamford, Lincolnshire, provide the ideal venue. Two World and three European Championships, including that of 1977, have been held here.

As a rule the steeplechase has little influence on the overall result because it is run on the top of the ground and it is very easy for the horses to go round and achieve maximum bonus. An exception was 1976, when the course was moved from the golf-course to a stubble area because of earlier heavy rain.

At Burghley it is specially important to be certain that the horse's rhythm is pronounced at the start of the cross country, then you can quietly accelerate. The fences

Opposite
The lake at Badminton, a permanent feature of the Three Day Event course in Gloucestershire which always attracts the biggest group of spectators

Opposite
Hurdle racing at the
Middleburg Hunt's Glenwood
Park course

Right
Lucinda Prior-Palmer on
George, in the brilliant cross
country ride which contributed
to her overall victory at
Badminton in 1977. This was
a very popular result after
Lucinda's tragic luck the
previous year, when her
winning mount Wideawake
died after the presentation of
the victor's trophy.

are unquestionably more formidable and solid than several years ago. The Trout
Hatchery is probably the most famous obstacle and Lars Sederholm considers it is often a
deceitful fence. 'Many horses have come to grief here and I think about half of those
who have fallen did so because the footing has been unlevel.' In the 1974 World
Championship there was a very stiff entry fence and the sloping downhill approach made
the water meet competitors very severely. The horses were looking down into the pond
as they drew into the obstacle but had to jump well up into the air. This was the year
that Princess Anne staged a remarkable recovery, remaining limpet-fashion with
Goodwill when all seemed lost, as did Captain Mark Phillips on his way to finishing
second on Mrs J. R. Hodgson's Gretna Green in 1975.

Since their debut at Chatsworth, the Midland Bank Championships moved to

Wylye, then Cirencester, and then Goodwood. From the start, the plan was to hold them for several years at a venue in a different part of the country: in 1977, a move was made northwards to Captain Patrick Drury Lowe's Locko Park, on the outskirts of Derby. This venue, founded only in 1975, has something of the Badminton/Burghley aura and much of its success can be attributed to the choice of Bob Hodgson, father of Janet, as course-builder.

A former M.F.H. of the Meynell and South Staffordshire, Bob Hodgson's aim was to build a solid cross country course. He spared neither time nor effort in designing what has proved a most popular challenge. For the first competition, British Horse Society course-builder Noel Palmer arrived with a repair gang in case of incident. Bob Hodgson greeted him, 'If you are ever needed, I shall give up.'

The riders who have made the journey to Scotland for Eglinton and Annick (Ayrshire), and Lockerbie (Dumfriesshire), which take place over eight days in August, speak highly of the friendly welcome and relaxing atmosphere. These events now have water obstacles and are considered just right for bringing on younger horses. Lord Strathclyde's Eglinton has the most timber, while Mr and Mrs M. R. Quarm's Annick, with views across the sea to the Isle of Arran, makes much use of natural hedges and ditches. Captain J. Bell Irving's Lockerbie, in the Valley of the Water of the Milk, is the most professional course of the three, built specifically for the occasion.

There are many really useful One Day Events suitable for novices at different stages of their education by virtue of terrain and jump-construction. Everdon near Daventry, Northamptonshire, which was originally a spring trial but is now held in late August, is an excellent meeting with first class organization. It is directed by the owner, Captain Dick Hawkins, a Joint Master of the Grafton, in the park surrounding Everdon Hall. The entire event is designed to produce a fair outing for both horse and rider. The hunting-type course is quite tough, a good novice is necessary and a cob is unlikely to be in the money because of the very steep hill in the farmland section. This event is always singled out by Olympic Gold Medallist Major Derek Allhusen for his young horses.

After a number of years as a Two Day Event, Michael Foljambe's Osberton fixture, held in August in the park surrounding his Regency house between Retford and Worksop, was expanded into a Three Day Event in 1977. There are some demanding jumps and the trials have a pleasing atmosphere. Because of the time of year, August, and good drainage, it is usually really firm and thus a real test of soundness. It is frequently chosen as a work-out for the final selection of the British Team and has some searching water-jumps.

Lord and Lady Hugh Russell's Open and Novice Three Day Event, held on their farm high above the Wylye Valley, is run quite magnificently. They regularly take a mammoth entry, often including foreign riders, in their stride with clockwork efficiency. The stubble fields and odd stones lying about can make this a very bleak experience on a wet, grey day, but there is probably no place in Britain with a greater variety of well built fences or better spectator visibility.

One of the last events in the calendar, Chatsworth, held in mid-October, with its incomparable Derwent Valley setting in Derbyshire, is an old favourite, much valued because it provides a yardstick for horses destined to make their debut at Badminton the following spring. It is the type of course where the size of the jumps is not too worrying

Opposite
Captain Mark Phillips on The Queen's Columbus in an event at Liphook in southern England. Columbus was winner at Badminton in 1974 with Captain Phillips, but later dropped out of eventing thanks to a tendon slipping off a hock. In 1977, however, Captain Phillips was able to ride him in Team Cross Country events and hunter trials.

as you walk round, but at the end of the day there have always been well spread stops and falls, the sign of a good course, rather than a concentration of all the problems at one fence. With its steep hill and sharp descents, Chatsworth places the stress on fitness and is full of variety in both terrain and obstacles. There are two spectacular water jumps, the Ice Pond on the side of the hill and Queen Mary's Bower, a small, moated tower near the river, where Mary Queen of Scots was imprisoned. Time and again this old, well tried course has proved that if a horse goes well here, it has a fair degree of both stamina and speed and is a likely Badminton contender.

Because of the stresses and strains of the sport, the competitive career of event horses is limited. Most English course-builders are well aware that it is vital not to damage the horse, and know how best to avoid doing so. In the past there used to be too many drops, which place enormous strain on the horses' tendons and can easily jar their backs. Landings are now far less often sited in depressions or on treacherously uneven or rough ground. It is also quite undesirable to hold the steeplechase phase on a sand track such as that for the 1976 Olympics at Bromont. Sandy going is dead and does not provide spring for take-off, or absorb the continual shock of landing like established, old turf.

In the cross country phase the horses' legs must be safeguarded to prevent elimination through injury. The aim in championships should be for as many teams to finish as possible. Since World War II, cross country courses have gradually become less severe. A much higher proportion of teams finished at the Munich Games (1972) than at Stockholm (1956) or Rome (1960). Trappy water as in Mexico (1968) and unfirm banks are also to be avoided at all costs.

A comparatively small course can be very deceptive, especially if, as at Bromont, there is constantly altering terrain with sharp turns, inclines and occasional rough surfaces, stones, roots of trees and boggy patches which prevent the horse establishing his stride and rhythm. Fortunately this type of ground is seldom used.

Bound fences were very much in vogue in the mid-1970s. The Chevrons and Star (Badminton, 1976) and the Witch Way and Apiary (Burghley, 1976) are in this category. A 'bounce' is definable as an obstacle with no canter stride between the two jumping elements. Distances range from 9 to 14ft (2.70-4.30m). The Star fence (Badminton, 1976) requires the ability to shorten and lengthen the stride, perfectly demonstrated by 1975 European Champion Lucinda Prior-Palmer on the bold and gay Wideawake on her way to victory. A horse of enormous scope may bounce a fence beyond the ability or contemplation of his rivals; I understand that Princess Anne's limitless Goodwill was bounced successfully through the rather longer Sunken Road at Badminton.

Another recent development at events such as Badminton and Burghley, where there are no steep hills, is the arranging of a group of obstacles, some of them combinations or bounces, so that the maximum number can be seen from the same viewing area. In eventing, one of the fastest developing sports in Europe, the course-builders are therefore wasting few chances of making competitions even more attractive for the spectators.

Eventing in North America
Sally O'Connor

Eventing is enjoying an unprecedented boom on the North American continent, both in the United States and in Canada. The numbers of those interested in the sport grow daily.

This growth developed in three distinct phases. To begin with, eventing was carried on exclusively by the military riders of the US Army. At the beginning of the century, the US Cavalry trained men and horses for use in battle, and when the equestrian events became part of the Olympic Games, at Stockholm in 1912, an American team was sent, finishing in third place behind the Swedish and Germans. Officers stationed in Europe took part in competition there, although the 'Military Event', as it was known in those days, was very different from the sport we know today. Tremendous distances were covered on the endurance portion, and the dressage test included galloping, pirouettes and jumping! Only 15 horses out of the 27 starters in the first Olympic Games managed to survive the demands of the competition. The initial American success was not repeated until 1932, although an American rider, Sloan Doak, won the individual bronze medal in Paris in 1924. The competition for the Games of 1932 was held on the American West Coast, in California, but due to the vast distances involved and the world economic crisis, only six nations were able to send teams. The US team, captained by Lt-Col. Harry D. Chamberlin, and including Lt Earl Thomson on the great mare Jenny Camp, and Lt Argo, won the gold medal, the Dutch being the only other team to finish three riders. Earl Thomson took the individual silver for the US. The last Olympics before World War II, held in Berlin and designed as a showcase for Nazi Germany, saw a controversial course for the Three Day which caused great difficulty. However Earl Thomson, promoted to Captain, rode Jenny Camp to the individual silver medal once again.

After the war the Games were resumed in London in 1948. For the last time the US Army fielded a team, consisting of Lt-Col. Frank Henry, who finished second to take the silver, Lt Charles Anderson, and the now Colonel, Earl Thomson.

The US Army through its Cavalry School at Fort Riley, Kansas, had provided the horses and training necessary for American riders to compete on equal terms with the Europeans. After demonstrating suitable talent, officers were stationed with the team, their sole duty being to ride and train horses. Officers on active duty gained valuable

experience from overseas postings, attending the famous schools of Europe at Saumur, in France, Tor di Quinto in Italy, and the cavalry school at Hanover. Brigadier General Jonathan R. Burton, who rode on the US Army teams during the period immediately following the war, credits the cavalry officers with bringing the forward seat and modern technique back from the European schools to the United States. In those early days, the captain of a team would serve also as coach. Every possible training facility existed at Fort Riley, including fences of every description, indoor riding-halls, dressage arenas and a permanent jumping-ring with all types of banks and ditches. But, outside of a few inter-regimental events, competition itself did not exist.

With the demise of the cavalry, the United States was faced with the problem of fielding teams in international competition. The transition to civilian status was rough indeed. The newly formed United States Equestrian Team (originally known as the International Equestrian Competitions Corporation) undertook the tremendous responsibility of getting teams together, and it was natural that those Army officers who had the knowledge and background be instrumental in the changeover. Colonel John W. Wofford at Fort Riley became the President of the infant USET. Jack Burton, then a Captain in the Army, was detailed to bring back some of the more experienced Army horses to the centre at Fort Riley. Although the Army was now mechanized, superb facilities were placed at the disposal of the USET. A one-man dynamo, Jack Burton

Above
Competitors in the Chicago Olympic Trials in 1947, including Lt-Col. Frank Henry (left) and Colonel Earl Thomson (second from right). Next to Frank Henry is Captain Jack Burton, now, as General Burton, head of the USET.

remained at Fort Riley to design and construct a suitable three-day course. 'It was an easy course by today's standards,' he recalls, 'but it contained just about all the different types of obstacles you met in those days, splashes, drops, banks, ditches. The construction was not as solid as it tends to be nowadays, the rails were thinner for instance, but I think we have a very representative course.'

There were horses, there was the course, the training facilities, but where were the riders? No civilian riders had any experience in the field of event riding. There were, however, many young men active in the showjumping world. Six of these were selected to train with Colonel Wofford. Among them, Walter Staley, Jr. recalls that none of them really understood what eventing entailed, and they were quickly overwhelmed by the amount of knowledge required. Under the tutelage of Colonel Wofford, who coached them for the cross country and jumping phases, and Captain Robert Borg, a former member of the Army dressage team, the six young men spent a busy year studying the skills needed to compete successfully in three-phase competition.

The course at Helsinki was generally accepted to be the most demanding seen to date in the Olympic Games. The young, untried team did creditably. With luck on their side, they finished all three riders, taking the bronze medal.

In a scant 14 months, an Olympic team had been developed from scratch. But it was readily apparent that there had to be more opportunity for developing horses and riders for this demanding sport, and the mid-1950s saw the first Three Day Event National Championship held in the Continental United States, the US teams participating in the Pan-American Games in Mexico in 1955. The team took no medals, although Walter Staley took home the individual gold.

The USET was doing its job in financing and training teams for international competition quite successfully. But there was still little opportunity for riders to develop horses through participation in competition on their own ground. Aspiring riders were forced to go to Europe to gain vital experience. One of these, Michael Page, spent 14 months at Saumur, and was one of the first civilians admitted to the formidable Cavalry School there. Americans were buying experienced horses from the Europeans and English, because of the lack in their own country. Among these was Copper Coin, the fantastic little horse trained by Ian Dudgeon, who was purchased for the US by John Galvin of California.

Mike Page was competing actively in the European events and this was brought to the attention of the USET. An offer of a horse to ride brought Mike back to the States. Paired with Grasshopper, the renamed little Irish horse, he chalked up success after success, winning individual gold medals in the Chicago and Sao Paulo Pan Am Games, and two silver team medals in the Rome and Tokyo Olympic Games, with an individual bronze in Tokyo. Here again was a horse developed in Europe, being ridden by a rider trained in Europe.

By the end of the 1950s it was evident that some sort of organization was needed to sponsor and regulate competition on the American continent. Modelled on the parent British organization, the US Pony Club was to play a dominant role in the development of three-phase competition and young riding talent. Finally, in 1959, a group of interested competitors organized the United States Combined Training Association. For the first time, America had the machinery by which to organize competitions at the

lowest levels in order to develop American horses and riders on this side of the Atlantic. There was no overnight miracle however, and for the first ten years progress was slow and erratic.

Apart from a handful of experienced international riders, no-one had seriously studied course design, and some weird and wonderful jumps came into being. The courses that did evolve were variable in quality. The tremendous variety of terrain and climate, and the vast size of the country, added to the difficulties. California, blessed with an almost ideal climate, developed one of the earlier good courses—the location at Pebble Beach, on the Pacific coast, has to be one of the most beautiful in the world. Gently rolling, with light soil, it offers the perfect footing for eventing, and breathtaking views out across the ocean. Dick Collins was responsible for a challenging but fair course.

The southern events developed slowly from the old army days, and most of them were founded close to an army base. The season was early in the year, before the heat made endurance well nigh impossible. In Virginia and Maryland, the traditional stronghold of foxhunting and steeplechasing, the country lent itself to more galloping-type courses. In Virginia the early obstacles were not as challenging as they could have been, offering the type of fences native to the local hunt country. Apart from one or two really eye-opening Advanced fences, they did not progress very far for several years, and many fences tended to be trappy in the extreme.

However, this area developed the first real circuit of spring and fall horse trials. Lower level competitions were used as an introduction to the sport and named 'Jenny Camp competitions', after Earl Thomson's gallant mare. These were either scaled-down versions of horse trials proper, or included a dressage ride and stadium course only. Even though the early courses were covered by the same rules and requirements, they varied wildly. Few people had any real feel for course design. Terrain differed from one part of the country to another; climate played a large role, with the sun baking the ground to a concrete consistency in summer, and the winter frosts making the ground unusable in winter.

One of the oldest Three Day Events in the country is held in late summer at the Green Mountain Horse Association in Vermont. Here terrain plays a vital part in the degree of difficulty of the course. A horse needs to be super fit to negotiate 'the mountain'. In the early days of the event, the roads and tracks went straight uphill for four miles or so to the course on top of a high mountain. This became a severe test of fitness. The veterinary check was all-important; horses unused to the climb could not complete the competitions. Course-design had little formal structure in those days, and the Vermont mountains lend themselves naturally to many drop fences. 'Stone walls and drops' was about the extent of the early GMHA courses, sometimes more suited to mountain goats than big, galloping horses.

The summer circuit led from Vermont up into Canada—a few enthusiasts were trying to get things started in that country. Ian Angus of Montreal developed a fine course, hosting a Three Day Event two weeks after the GMHA. The only flaw was a lack of space in which to develop the course, so that it tended to double back on itself rather too often. The fences were big and solid, and well sited in natural country.

The Canadians managed to field a team of riders for the Olympic Games in

Previous page
Bruce Davidson and Easy Payment on the cross country course of a pony club trials at Redlands in the spring of 1976

Above
Chris Ayers on The Senator at
the Flying Horse Three Day
Event at South Hamilton,
Massachusetts, in 1976

Stockholm, which managed an astounding third-place finish. Jim Elder, a member of the jumping team as well as the three day squad, recalls that 'we had a great deal of luck going for us. We had horses that had little or no experience except in hunting and racing, but they managed to survive the cross country in one piece, which made up for some disastrous dressage scores.' Progress in Canada was also hindered by the fact that the ground is frozen generally until mid-June. The Pony Clubs were beginning to develop courses at the lower levels. An annual National Rally was moved to a different part of the country each year, and each time a new course was built. This led to the construction of sensible lower level courses, although not without some bad mistakes being made.

Throughout the 1950s and 60s the sport gradually evolved, but there was still a lack of opportunity to develop truly international horses and riders in competition. There were only a handful of advanced riders. Most of the experienced horses were imports from Europe. Women had been traditionally considered unable to stand up to the rigours of the three day endurance phases. But it was becoming increasingly apparent that they could compete on equal terms with their male counterparts. By 1964, they were becoming increasingly active in the sport, both in Europe, where Sheila Willcox had won the European Championship, and in the United States. The FEI regulations were amended in time to allow women to ride in the Olympic Games in Tokyo. Lana Dupont of the United States, riding a home-bred thoroughbred gelding, Mister Wister, was the first woman ever to ride in an Olympic competition, paving the way for countless others following in her footsteps.

The early riders were coached by the army officers they were replacing. However, problems within the USET found the three day squad without a coach at the beginning of the season leading up to the Olympic Games in 1968. Major Joe Lynch was drafted as a last minute replacement. He recollects walking into the barn at Gladstone, New Jersey, training headquarters for the USET, and looking down the row of horses in the stables. With few exceptions, they were old friends he had known and helped develop in Europe. J. Michael Plumb, a rider who had been on the US team in Rome, and Tokyo, remembers the course in Mexico with mixed feelings. 'Some of the fences were not even finished by the time we arrived, and the footing was badly affected by the torrential rains that fell. The water fences were transformed into a rider's nightmare by the swift streams.' He feels that stringent control should be exercised on the development of courses for the Olympic Games. 'The English courses at Badminton and Burghley are the sort of courses that should be used for the Games.'

Michael Plumb, Kevin Freeman, Jim Wofford and Michael Page typify the riders developed in the period after the army teams no longer represented the US. With minimum guidance, they developed their own skills. Travelling to competitions abroad, they gradually developed their talent, and took their places with world-class riders from other nations. None of them had the advantage of early training from Pony Club, because Pony Club didn't exist. They came into the sport from riding cross country, hunting or racing. In both Tokyo and Mexico the team finished in second place, with Mike Page taking the individual bronze in Mexico.

The year following the Mexico Olympics, 1969, two men who were to have a revolutionary effect on the sport in the United States took separate, but closely related jobs. First there was Neil Ayer, M.F.H., avid polo-player and an eventing enthusiast, who took over the Presidency of the USCTA. Neil Ayer had long been interested in the development of the sport, and had a taste for course design and building. Neil set to work with boundless enthusiasm, and a flair for organization. Providing strong leadership, endless energy, and a well run central office that functioned as a clearing house for all parts of the country, he set out to transform the USCTA into an integral whole. A progression of trials was set up, a circuit from early trials in the south on to the important major events in late summer and late fall further north.

In Jack Le Goff, former French team medallist and instructor at the Saumur Cavalry Schools, the USET found the ideal coach. His thorough background and detailed knowledge of all aspects of the sport brought about a revolution, both in course design

Opposite
Mike Plumb and Good Mixture on the cross country course at the Middletown, Delaware, Pony Club. Plumb was a member of the US Olympic Gold Team in 1976 and individual silver medallist.

and theory, and in the development of young riders and horses. Under his influence, the first really world-class American courses began to take shape. At her family home in Fair Hill, Maryland, Jean Dupont McConnell undertook to construct a course of championship calibre. Already famed for its steeplechase meets, the existing stabling and racecourse offered ready-made facilities for part of a major Three Day Event. Big imposing fences, designed to test the mettle of the bold horse, were built on the rolling hills of northern Maryland. Patterned after the combination of banks crossing the road at the Rome Olympics, the triple-bank combination quickly became the focal point of interest 'for riders.

Interest in course design was growing throughout the country, aided by the developing talents of Richard Newton, then at the Potomac Horse Center, by Jack Le Goff's course at Midland, Georgia, and Roger Haller's achievements in building the Essex Three Day courses. Rules and regulations for participation were revised. The doldrums were passed, new horizons appeared.

In Canada also, whole communities became involved, with towns getting behind the efforts of local organizers. Dunham in Quebec sponsored a major Three Day competition. At Joker's Hill in Ontario, courses were developed for the eastern Canadian Championships. In Alberta and British Columbia new events developed and flourished.

Opposite
This substantial obstacle is typical of those found on the Training Level courses of American Pony Clubs

Below
Jimmy Wofford on Grey Friar at the Blue Ridge Two Day Event in Virginia, 1976

For as long as he can remember, Bruce Davidson has had a keen interest in horses. Attending a military school in Maryland, he participated in the riding programme, quickly rising to become captain of the team. 'I had always ridden cross country, hunting and jumping,' he recalls, 'but I didn't have any serious lessons except what I got as a Pony Clubber.' Determined to make a career of riding, Bruce decided to try his luck at the screening trials run by USET Coach Bertalan De Nemethy in 1969. His usual horse had gone lame and Bruce had nothing to ride but an older brood mare, six months in foal.

Bruce confesses that he wasn't quite sure what was expected at the screening. 'The first day we spent doing flat work. I didn't really know much about it. At the end of the day De Nemethy called me to the side of the ring. "Do you know *anything?*" he asked. All I had been doing was trotting around. However, he was sufficiently impressed with the jumping on the next day for him to ask where my interest lay.' In the fall he reported to the USET training quarters in Gladstone to begin work with Le Goff. He vividly remembers his first meeting with the new coach. 'I had driven my horse to the stables and then gone on up to Massachusetts to my home. I drove up and back, a seven-hour trip. My tack trunk was locked in another car and I was due at the first session. Jumping onto my horse with only a halter and lead shank I set off hurriedly for the training grounds. Riding around a corner I nearly knocked someone flat—it was Mr Le Goff! Not a very promising introduction.'

With a borrowed horse, Bruce spent the summer working with Jack Le Goff, learning just how much he had to learn. Long hours spent in the saddle slowly developed his ability both on the flat and over fences. In early September Bruce went on an extended hunt for horses with Gabor Foltenyi, a former Hungarian event rider who had the reputation of finding and turning out exceptionally fine prospects. After looking at literally hundreds of horses Bruce finally found what he had been looking for in Ohio. The horse was a big, bay, thoroughbred gelding, six years old and recently broken in. It was Irish Cap.

From then on Bruce and 'Cappy' were living at Gladstone, Bruce riding the experienced team horses and developing his own young horse under Le Goff's expert tutelage. A year of competition followed. In the fall of 1971, riding the veteran Plain Sailing, Bruce won the Eastern Canadian Championships in Montreal. The following winter, Bruce was again selected to work at Gladstone for another intensive training period, putting together a style and technique that were to stand him in good stead in the years ahead.

In 1972, an Olympic year, a virulent disease was sweeping the North American continent, an equine encephalitis imported from South America. European nations were closing their borders to American horses. To comply with the quarantine regulations enforced in Europe during the dangerous season, horses and riders flew to England to prepare in the spring season there, with an eye on the Olympic Games in Munich.

Bruce was expecting the English courses to be 'astronomically big' by comparison with the ones he knew. In fact they were not too different after all—'until I got to Badminton and saw that course. It's the sort of course that makes tingles run down your spine. This is what it should be. This is it. I wondered how the Olympics could beat this.' However, he found the course in Munich to be well built, a galloping course, in

Opposite
World Champion Bruce Davidson and Golden Griffin at the Pan Am Games, Mexico City, 1975

fact a 'runaway' course, which is just what Plain Sailing nearly did with him. Runaway
or no, Bruce was on the team that took home yet another silver medal.

Courses were ever improving back in the US. That built for the first Ledyard
International in 1973 was challenging and big. 'It was more of a technical course in that
it couldn't compare with the big galloping courses at Badminton and Burghley, but
provided the rider with problems of approach and judgement.' It was a 'rider's course', a
good example of an American course as opposed to big straightforward English courses,
and represented a stage in the evolution of the sport in America.

By 1974 Bruce was well established. Riding the team horses he had been successful
in every competition entered; at the same time he was developing his own Irish Cap as a
strong contender in the lower levels. In early 1974 he married Carol Hannum, another
event rider with her own horses in top competition. Taking their horses with them, they
flew to England to spend their honeymoon on the spring event circuit there. Cappy came
third at Badminton, assuring Bruce a place on the World Championship team for the
big event at Burghley later in the year.

The riders that went to Burghley were a mixture of veterans and new riders. Mike
Plumb, who had ridden in from Olympic Games, winning three silver team medals,
had the ride on Good Mixture, a horse developed by Kevin Freeman and an experienced
campaigner. A difficult horse to get along with, shy and mistrustful, Good Mixture is
nonetheless a first-class cross-country horse. Denny Emerson had developed his own
little horse Victor Deakin, but was without much international experience. Don Sachey,
a young rider selected through the USET screenings, rode the veteran Plain Sailing, a
great team horse, who provided much-needed training for many young riders. The team
was completed by two young girls chosen through the screenings held in previous years,
Beth Perkins of Vermont with the former Australian horse, Furtive, and Caroline
Treviranus, on a home-bred mare with very little experience in world class competition.

The results are in the history books. Bruce Davidson and Irish Cap lived up to their
promise and emerged as the new World Champions. Mike Plumb, pushing at his team-
mate's heels, won yet another silver medal. Beth Perkins finished in sixth place overall.
The team took the gold medals home.

The lone Canadian rider at Burghley, Juliet Graham, deserves equal praise. Riding her grey mare, Sumatra, a notoriously difficult horse on the flat, but with an indomitable spirit cross country, she was far off the pace after the first phase, but with a scorching round improved her position to eighth overall, sandwiched between Richard Meade and Bridget Parker. Without the backing of a strong organization such as the USCTA, Canadian riders developed themselves against great odds.

The USET headquarters at Gladstone were seriously overcrowded with the influx of Three Day horses, in addition to the Prix des Nations horses. Coach De Nemethy and Jack Le Goff were hard put to find enough time to work all the various riders and horses in separate sessions. In 1974 Forrester A. 'Tim' Clark generously donated a large horse facility in Hamilton, Massachusetts to the USET, specifically for the use of the Three Day team.

The Three Day horses and riders made the move north after the victory in Burghley. For the first time, the event team had available all the necessary training facilities, a steeplechase course at Flying Horse Farm, and not one, but two, great cross country courses, Flying Horse and the innumerable fences at Ledyard. A large indoor ring was constructed to make wintertime riding in the frosty Massachusetts winters possible.

A true indication of the growth of the sport, Fox Hollow Farm at Hamilton not only houses the Three Day riders, but provides an office for General Jack Burton, retired from the Army and acting as the Vice-President of the USET. Close to the sport that he loves, he played an active role in developing the new training centre.

In 1974 the first North American Junior Championships were hosted by the Joker's Hill event in Ontario. Eight teams, from the US and from Canada, vied for top honours. The host team from Ontario were the eventual winners. All involved were agreed that this competition was a great step in the development of young riders. Indeed, as more and more children have graduated out of the US and Canadian Pony Clubs, the general levels of competition have steadily risen. In 1975 Canada again played host, with a team from the US the winners. In 1976 the competition moved to the United States, and a new course designed and built in the mid-section of the country, Illinois. Competition among young riders is becoming intense. Both countries are developing strong young riders from which potential international teams can be drawn in the future. In 1976, there were over 200 competitions at various levels, a far cry from the 21 in 1965.

The annual competition for the longer established US National Junior Championships was lucky to attract 10 or 12 riders in the 1950s and 60s. For the past few years the numbers have steadily grown and now it is taken for granted that there will be over 60 young riders eligible for the competition. Most of these have come from Pony Club ranks. Held over a moderately difficult Preliminary course, the Junior Championship takes the form of a full Three Day Event, and many of the hopefuls for the international teams have come from their ranks.

Notable among these is Tad Coffin, who has been working with Jack Le Goff at the USET headquarters since 1973. Developing his abilities through riding both the team horses and his own two young horses, he has followed much the same path as Bruce Davidson, Le Goff slowly building up his skills and talent. Partnered with the team's great mare, Bally Cor, Tad finished fourth at Ledyard in 1975 and then went on to win

Opposite
A happy landing for Evie Thorndike and Royal Beaver at the Swimming Pool, Ledyard International, 1975

the gold medal in the Pan American Games in Mexico.

Ledyard was again designated as a CCI (*Concours Complet d'Equitation*, the official term for an international event) in 1975. Moved up to a date in June because of the preparation for the Pan American Games, it was a truly international event, attracting British, German, Dutch and Canadian riders besides the Americans. Great interest was occasioned by the presence of Princess Anne and her husband Mark Phillips. Thousands of spectators thronged to watch the excitement. Bruce Davidson felt that the course had been greatly improved since 1973. 'There was a great effort to make it more straightforward, an attempt to make it a more galloping course. It was a good compromise between a galloping course, and the previous technical course.' It obviously suited Bruce. He was placed first and third on Golden Griffin and Royal Cor, both team horses. (Irish Cap had suffered a debilitating lung infection and was out of work for a whole year.) The Canadian riders, too, were there in force, trying hard to catch up with the Americans in experience and horses. They were prominent in the lower divisions, riding several nice young, but green, horses.

In 1975 the Canadians were making a concentrated effort to develop their young riders. They showed up at many of the US spring trials. A team of four riders was sent to Mexico, made up of Peter Howard on Deep South, formerly ridden by Jim Day, Liz Ashton, another Canadian who rides for both the jumping team and the Three Day Squad, Jim Day, gaining quite a reputation in this new discipline, and Jim Henry on the English bred Law and Order. After the dressage day, the US stood in first place, Mexico second and the Canadians third, with Guatemala fourth. The cross country was twisting and on difficult terrain. A very steep slide looked quite terrifying to the riders walking the course, but as it turned out it caused little difficulty, and the competition was rather a comedy of errors as far as the officiating went.

The United States finished in first place. The team was made up entirely of the younger riders brought along by Le Goff—Bruce Davidson, Tad Coffin, Beth Perkins and a newcomer, in her second international event, Mary Anne Tauskey. The Canadians, in spite of Jim Day's unfortunate elimination, did well enough to win the silver team medal. Tad Coffin on Bally Cor won the individual gold, with Bruce, in spite of a fall, taking home the silver.

The Canadian eventing world had been split into various groups, but with the prospect of hosting the Olympic Games, and competing on home ground, a concentrated effort was made to heal the divisions. At the beginning of 1976 a first class coach was hired, in the person of Mike Page, former medallist for the US. Under his direction horses and riders moved south to Florida for the winter and followed the spring circuit up into Virginia and Maryland.

Jim Day, from Ontario, was a relative newcomer to the sport. A member of the Prix des Nations squad, he had several medals to his credit as a showjumping rider. He won the individual gold medal in the 1967 Pan American Games, with the Canadians taking the team bronze; was a member of the gold medal team in the 1968 Olympics and the 1970 World Championships in France; and rode on the team in Munich in 1972. It was while he was in Munich that he took a closer look at the Three Day Event competition, and decided that 'it was a natural'. Starting his eventing career in 1973, he found 'it was a bigger job than I had anticipated. There was a lot more to it than I realized.' There

Opposite
Princess Anne and Arthur of Troy negotiating the notorious Ledyard Coffin at the Ledyard International Event of 1975

Above
Essex, New Jersey, Horse
Trials, spring 1974: Lornie
Forbes and Story Time leaping
the bullfinch in heavy rain

were few events in Canada in which to improve his skills, but he did well enough to win the North American Championship at Joker's Hill, riding Deep South. He acknowledges the fact that although Canada has one or two first class full three day competitions, it lacks the broad structure of events that has grown up in the United States, and which enables American riders to bring their horses along slowly and logically.

The spring of 1976 was a mini-preview of the competition to come at the Games. Not only the Canadians and Americans were preparing themselves, but also the Japanese team who had been in America for a year in order to gain much needed experience. The colours of all three nations showed up regularly throughout the early months.

The USCTA organized a series of selection trials so that the USET could draw up a short list of riders for the Games. At each trial there were two separate divisions at the advanced level, one for declared candidates for the US team, and an open division. The Canadians dominated this second division.

The American short list at the end of these trials contained six names—Mike Plumb, Bruce Davidson, Tad Coffin, Denny Emerson, Mary Anne Tauskey and Beth Perkins. In announcing the names for the short list, General Jack Burton recalled the

Above
Bromont Olympics, 1976;
Richard Meade on Jacob Jones
at the second element of the
lake

days when 'we were scratching around for riders. Never before has there been such a wealth of talent to choose from, which made our job extremely difficult.' In his opinion, American had come a long way in a relatively short time. As hosts for the Games, the Canadians undertook the awesome task of designing and building the eventing course. They opted to build an entirely new one at the Bromont site. Course-designer Barbara Kemp, felt that cross country courses should traverse natural country, with obstacles being what you might expect to meet out riding. This was much the same philosophy as pervaded course design in the United States at the beginning of the 1960s. Courses have advanced a great deal since then.

The terrain at Bromont is hilly and quite rough. In places it was extremely hard and rocky, and varied greatly throughout the length of the course. The fences on the whole were well built, albeit flimsy at times, but the course lacked any sense of rhythm. Fences were of uneven difficulty, ranging from massive solid obstacles, to trappy, flimsy ones. Most of the riders agreed that it was not a true test of an event horse. Mike Plumb, having ridden over the courses in Rome, Tokyo, Mexico, and Munich, in addition to the best courses in England and America, had some things to say about the course in Bromont. In an interview for *Dressage* magazine he stated: 'It was a pony type, a billy-goat type of course. It didn't follow in the sport of three day eventing at all, in that most of the fences were not difficult at all, it was how you got to the fences. It's hard to put into words about that course, but it just never gave me a feeling of satisfaction . . . I'd like to know how some of the horses came out of this . . . I just wonder how generous they'll be with their stride after this event. Not only soundness-wise, there were a lot of horses hurt, but just the horses who tried 150 percent as mine did. I don't think there was any horse who tried harder than he, because he was dead tired at the end. I just wonder what his feeling is going to be the next time he goes on course, and I've got to give it a lot of thought that the first event I run him at is a galloping course and not one you have to jerk his teeth out every stride to get him right to a fence, or have a lot of rolling ground where he never finds where his foot is going to be . . . Next time, the person who designs the course should be someone who has either ridden, watched, or been involved with an Olympic level Three Day Event.' Bromont, unfortunately, was a step back in time for courses in North America.

The American team included two riders with international experience in Europe, Mike Plumb and Bruce Davidson, and two who had been trained in competition in North America, Tad Coffin and Mary Anne Tauskey. The horses, with the exception of Bruce's Irish Cap, received most of their experience entirely in competition at home. The eventual gold medal winner, Tad Coffin on Bally Cor, was riding an American-bred and American-trained horse, as was Mike Plumb with the relatively inexperienced Better and Better, a horse that had previously seen little advanced competition. The team gold medal was proof positive of the coaching genius of Jack Le Goff. In a few short years he had welded together a world-class team. His success lies in his attention to detail all through the year and in competition. To watch him at an important event gives a clue to his talent. He is omnipresent. Whenever a team member has a question, whenever a problem arises, the coach is there and he has the answers.

The Canadians are determined to produce riders of equal talent. The year 1976 saw the beginning of a concentrated effort on their part. Of their riders, Juliet Graham, who had developed herself in international competition, finished in 11th place overall at Bromont. Jim Day's Viceroy was well in the running but suffered an unfortunate injury and had to be retired after the endurance phases. Kathy Wedge was in fine shape until the very last fence, when the gruelling uphill finish took its toll and her horse had a crashing fall at the very last fence. With more luck on their side, the Canadians would have been in contention.

From its early military beginnings, through a typically rough adolescence, the eventing in North America has grown and matured. A tremendous surge of interest has followed the victories at Burghley and Bromont. Americans are competitive—they like to win.

As host of the World Championship in Kentucky in 1978, the United States is sparing no effort to build a championship-calibre course that rivals the best in the world. The site offers first-class facilities and perfect footing. With typical American energy and enthusiasm, the sport of cross country riding has been developed to take its place as one of the most exciting sports in the country. In the years ahead Americans, and Canadians too, are determined to take their place alongside the best in the world.

Eventing on the Continent of Europe

Findlay Davidson

The entire sport of eventing owes its origin largely to the Cavalry Schools of Europe at the end of the last century, and in the early years of the 20th; for it was from the long-distance rides then undertaken by the cavalry that eventing evolved.

Today the Cavalry Schools have all been closed, and major influences are the use of thoroughbred, or near-thoroughbred stock, the Junior European Horse Trials Championships, and, to quite a surprising extent, Princess Anne.

When the Princess first competed at the Dutch Three Day Event at Boekelo, not far from the German border, I was told of two worthy old ladies, who, having paid to park their car and also for admittance, saw her going out on the first roads and tracks. This was within five minutes of their arrival, and they then turned and went away satisfied. Of course, not many people are like that, but many of those who have come for such a reason have also enjoyed themselves, and returned another year, bringing in the money that the sport needs to survive.

No country on the Continent of Europe has one overall sponsor for events, unlike Britain where the vast majority are under the sponsorship of the Midland Bank. In West Germany, the National Federation lays down the amount of prize money that must be given for the various levels of event, but the organizer concerned has to find this sum from sponsors or his public.

In the days of the long-distance ride, this was one problem that the organization did not have to deal with. Instead, however, the logistics of the organized long-distance ride must have often caused Army officers as many problems as the Three Day Event secretary of today has to face. One of the more famous of these rides was run from Vienna to Berlin in October 1892, finishing at Tempelhof. The time taken for this distance, about 370 miles, was 71 hr 26 min. Forty-two of the 98 starters, all of them officers of the Austrian, German and Hungarian Armies, finished. The average speed of the winner, Count Lt Wilhelm Starhemberg, was 5.17 mph. The winner apparently trained for this event with daily 30-mile rides.

The Belgians and the French also went in for distance rides, including one from Brussels to Ostend, a distance of 85.5 miles being covered in around seven hours. The French had the distinction of having the longest ride, from Biarritz to Paris, about 450 miles.

At the beginning of this century various countries were evolving a test that resembles the modern Three Day Event. One of the first was the *Championnat du Cheval d'Armes* which started in Paris with a dressage test on 29 March 1902. Thirty-three starters completed this and went on to tackle a 2½-mile steeplechase which had to be covered in under nine minutes. Then followed a 31-mile equivalent of the modern roads and tracks, to be followed after a rest day with showjumping in the Grand Palais. The winner, from the Second Hussars, was a Lieutenant de Saint-Phalle, well known at that time for his dressage ability, on a thoroughbred, Marseille II. This event is the direct antecedent of the French *Championnat de Concours Complet d'Equitation* still held today.

These and many other distance rides led to a proposal to include equestrian events other than polo in the 1908 Olympics. This did not happen, but the Games in Stockholm in 1912 did include what might be called a four-phase event. Run over four days, this comprised a long-distance ride of some 34 miles, of which 3 miles were over a cross country course, the whole to be covered in 4 hours. On the second day there was a 2.2 mile steeplechase, followed on the third day by jumping, and on the fourth by dressage.

The cross country course itself had to be covered in 15 minutes, 130 marks being allocated to this phase, with a deduction of 2 for an initial refusal, or 5 for a second refusal or fall of either rider or horse. Two marks were knocked off for each five seconds over time. The long-distance ride had a 10 mark maximum awarded to it, with one mark being deducted for each minute or part of a minute over the time. The steeplechase similarly had 10 marks with deductions as for the cross country, except that 2 were removed for each second over the time allowed of 5 minutes 50 seconds. The showjumping could have given a rider 150 marks and the dressage a massive 770, a complete imbalance compared with the modern event. The winner of this first Olympic Three Day Event was Lt Axel Nordlander, a Swede, riding Lady Artist. The Swedes also won the team gold, but they owed both medals to their superior dressage achievements. The German team took the silver, USA the bronze, and France was fourth. Belgium, Denmark and Great Britain were all eliminated.

The Swedes repeated their feat of winning both gold medals at Antwerp in 1920, but in Paris in 1924 they had to be content with the team silver. At this latter event the rules started to resemble those of today, and the relative importance of the three phases of dressage, endurance and jumping became 2 : 12 : 4. It was the Dutch that wrested the team gold from the Swedes, and their Lt A. van der Voort van Zip on Silver Prince who took the individual gold. Seventeen teams took part in 1924 and in 1928 in Amsterdam this number had gone up to 20, but with each team composed of three individuals instead of four as previously. Once again it was the Dutch that were successful for both the team and the individual gold, Lt C. F. Pahud de Mortanges on Marcroix finishing ahead of his compatriot, Captain de Kruyff.

De Mortanges and Marcroix went on to gain the gold in Los Angeles in 1932, the first and only time, to date, that anyone has achieved an Olympic double in this sport.

The Berlin Olympics of 1936 will be remembered for the Teutonic thoroughness of the organization and the fourth fence of the cross country course, a low post-and-rails with a small lake on the landing side. Of the 46 horses that jumped this fence, 18 fell and a further 10 unseated their riders. Overnight rain had caused the level of the water

in the lake to be higher than anticipated, but the main problem appeared to be that the lake bottom sloped away rather more than expected. The crowd was certainly the largest to have appeared at an event up to that time, and once they discovered the source of the trouble, by sheer weight of numbers they were able to stop loose horses going too far. Unfortunately one animal was put down at the lake and two fatalities occurred on the course. Luckily the power of the technical delegate seems to have been greater at subsequent Olympic Games. As was almost to be expected, the Germans won the gold team, and their Captain Ludwig Stubbendorf, on Nurmi, gained the individual gold.

Although riders from eleven European countries were amongst those who contested the 1948 Olympic event, held in Britain, the games of 1952 in Helsinki saw virtually a new beginning to this sport in Europe. Helsinki saw the entry of the civilian rider into the sport and into the medals. The course on sandy, stony ground was generally reckoned to have been on the severe side, only six of the 19 teams that started finishing. Sweden took the team gold and their Hans von Blixen-Finecke, on Jubal, the individual gold.

In 1953 the first European Championships were held at Badminton. As only three teams participated the team title could not be awarded (a minimum of four teams is necessary) but the British team won the unofficial contest, the Irish and Swiss teams failing to finish. Major Lawrence Rook on Starlight and Major Frank Weldon on Kilbarry took the first two individual placings for Britain. This was the start of an unbroken series of international victories for Britain, that went on until 1959, when the Germans gained the gold at Harewood. The British later repeated this performance during the period 1967 to 1972, when they gained every team championship at official internationals and the majority of those at friendly contests, before going down, to the West Germans, at Kiev in 1973.

It became evident, when only five teams came forward in May 1955, that spring was the wrong time of the year for a European championship due to the difficulties of getting horses fit on the Continent where snow is so often a training problem. That autumn an event was held in Turin where Sheila Willcox was successful with High and Mighty. The British team was first, with the Germans second. Included in the German team was Alwin Schockemöhle on Lausbub. Twenty years later he was to win the European Show Jumping Championship in Munich and the following year the individual gold medal for showjumping at the Montreal Olympics. It is interesting to note that several of the top German showjumping riders have international eventing experience, a phenomenon that has also occurred amongst the French and Italians.

Because of Australian quarantine regulations, the equestrian events of the Melbourne Olympics were held in Stockholm in 1956. Nineteen countries took part, with 56 competitors, and they faced a cross country course made severer by a day of solid rain. Several of the fences on slopes became particularly difficult, notably a trakehner with steep slopes on each side at Fence 22. Here the Swedish horse Iller broke a leg, and Bertie Hill got stuck with HM the Queen's Countryman III. However he got over it quite easily at the second attempt and went on to finish. The incident was not as serious for Britain as it could have been, for the team finally ended up with 120 penalties less than the West German team that was second. Petrus Kastenman, a Swedish Army

sergeant, won the individual gold with Illuster, having a margin of 15.33 penalties over Germany's August Lütke-Westhues.

The following year, in the European Championships in Copenhagen, Kastenman and Illuster were complete flops, running up 460 penalties on the cross country. This seemed to be the end of top class eventing and eventers in the whole of Scandinavia—yet every so often there comes a rider from that part of Europe to surprise everyone. One such was Jan Johnson who went well at Burghley in 1971 with Sarajevo, and very much better the following year in Munich, when he gained the Olympic bronze. Apart from the Junior European Championships at Holstebro in 1970, there has not been another international Three Day Event of any significance since in any of the Scandinavian countries. Those Junior Championships in Holstebro did provide another unique double. Nils-Olof Barkander, who won the individual award for Sweden on Pegasus, had the week before taken part in the Junior European Show Jumping Championships in St Moritz, where he had gone well enough to win one of the preliminary competitions. Petrus Kastenman has recently shown more interest in the sport internationally, being a spectator at Badminton in 1976, and assisting in the training of the two Swedish girls who took part in the Junior Championships of 1976 at Siekkrug in Northern Germany.

Currently in Denmark and Sweden there is very much a 'chicken and egg' situation, there being quite a number of riders and events at novice level; but as there are not enough of them with sufficient experience for higher level One Day Events, none are run, and the riders do not get the experience unless they go for some time to Britain or Germany, which few can afford.

But to hark back to Copenhagen in 1957. Sheila Willcox showed her Badminton form which High and Mighty, despite having 20 faults in the jumping phase, held in incessant rain (so heavy that no photographer braved the elements for the final presentation), to win fairly comfortably from August Lütke-Westhues on Franko II. The margin between the British and German teams was however noticeably less than in Basle or Stockholm.

No championships were held in 1958, when for the first time there was a winner from the Continent at the British autumn Three Day Event at Harewood in Yorkshire. This was Ottokar Pohlmann on Polarfuchs. He returned a year later to lead the West German team to victory. Now Herr Pohlmann is well known throughout Europe for his ability as a course-designer. Also in that German team was Reiner Klimke, who in 1974 won the World Dressage Championships in Copenhagen. In his book, *Military*, Dr Klimke points to the development of the One Day Event as being one of the keys to that German victory. The need for the rider to have his eye in for riding across country is one of the most important benefits of the One Day Event.

In 1976 in West Germany there were 73 One Day Events at novice level, seven at intermediate level, and two at advanced level with a total of 1832 starters amongst them. In addition there were 23 Two or Three Day Events with 641 starters. Both these totals were apparently on the low side, due mainly to the drought that affected the going throughout much of Europe in that long, hot summer. These figures are at much the same level as those in the United States where there were 1578 starters in the top five levels of competition. The USCTA shows a further 10,433 starters at lower levels, mainly riding club events, which are not noted by the German Federation or the British Horse Society's Combined Training Group. The latter show that 4880 horses started in their novice One or Two Day Events in 1976, with a further 1762 starting in intermediate or open intermediate classes, and 337 more in advanced classes. Add a further 202 for starters in junior trials, and 497 for the five Three Day Events in Britain and you get a massive figure of 7678 for the total number of event starts in the British Isles. It is no wonder then that virtually any Three Day Event in Europe that is open to them will see some British competitors. Back in 1959, the total starts made in Britain was well under the thousand mark. Assuming the German figures to be as low

proportionately, then the achievement of the West German team in winning at Harewood becomes that much greater. The winning margin, though, was just 0.3 penalties, which gave even greater interest to the next meeting of the two teams at the Rome Olympics of 1960.

The trials held by both Britain and Germany prior to Rome in each case gave the other side something to smile about. Australia's Bill Roycroft on Our Solo and Laurie Morgan on Salad Days finished first and second at Badminton to give the British more than a little to mull over. Then at Luhmühlen, the leading German rider was Hans Günther Winkler on Bellona. He had won a team gold in the 1956 Olympics on Halla and was to gain another that year.

Eighteen teams took part in Rome, and this time there was a reversion to the old rule of the best three of four to count. In all the reports there is mention of chaotic organization. There was no excuse for the lack of a bell or some other means of starting competitors in the dressage, or for the non-announcement of scores. The course was badly built, far too many fences being flimsy, so that they had to be rebuilt quite frequently during the course of the day. The take-offs and landings of several fences collapsed, a problem which the fence judges solved by moving flags. Well-thought-out plans of approach thus quickly had to be changed, which hardly led to peace of mind for competitors. Despite all this, the Australian team went well, although Brian Crago's Sabre had broken down. Bill Roycroft, in hospital with a broken shoulder, had to emerge to compete in the final jumping at the Piazza di Siena, home of the Rome Horse Show. He had a faultless round on Our Solo. Laurie Morgan on Salad Days returned the only plus score of the whole event, so the Australians were winners of team and individual golds, and also the individual silver. Switzerland, France, Great Britain, Italy and Ireland were the other finishing teams, in that order.

The Italian organization was not that much better when the Junior European Championships were held over much the same course in 1974. Many of the fences seemed unsuitable for a Junior Championship, so much so that the Dutch team captain withdrew his entire team before the cross country phase. He may well have been right too, for two horses were killed on the course.

There seems to be little eventing in Italy at the moment, and, when present, Italian teams have not fared very well at recent international events. When one considers the Italian interest in showjumping today it is indeed surprising that they do not do far better in eventing. However, they have been buying proven horses that could be suitable for the Junior Championships, so possibly more can be expected of them in the future.

In 1961 there were no European Championships. André le Goupil on Jacasse B won the French title, and Fritz Ligges took the German title on Föhn at Luhmühlen. He won there again in 1962 on Donkosak.

The European Championships were held in Britain at Burghley in 1962. For the first running of the Championships at the venue only four teams came forward. France and the USSR sent teams from the Continent and the Irish came as well, to make the minimum number. Surprisingly the Russian stallions, wiry looking thoroughbreds, went a lot better over the cross country course than had been expected and the Russian team won. Second was Ireland, with Britain and France trailing behind. James Templar on M'Lord Connolly was the individual winner, but was not in the British team.

Opposite
André le Goupil, 1961 French champion, riding Arthémise at Fontainebleau

Opposite, above and below
A perfect jump at the cross
country course at Dourdan in
France

It was three years before the European Championships were next held, in Moscow, but in the meantime there was a CCI at Munich in August 1963 when six nations took part in an unofficial team competition. Here the British were victorious with Poland second and Germany third. Templar, with M'Lord Connolly, was again successful individually. The Italians were eliminated when one of their riders took the wrong course during the showjumping, but they had shown some useful form.

Just how useful that form was, was seen in Japan, at Karuizawa, some 80 miles from Tokyo. Here the Italian team went exceptionally well over the cross country course, and their top three finished with a final score of ;A85.8. The United States, West Germany, Ireland, Russia, Argentina, Australia, France and Mexico finished in that order behind them. Mauro Checcoli on Surbean took the individual gold for Italy.

Although seven teams were entered at Moscow in 1965, only three were from the West, those of Ireland, Germany and Britain. The course was well built and suited the Irish very well; before the showjumping they were in the lead. However, the loss of 41 marks in the jumping phase cost them the team gold, the Russians with three clear rounds moving in instead. The individual gold also went to Russia.

In 1966 the first World Championships were held at Burghley with just five teams. Infectious equine anaemia, rampant in Western Europe, stopped all other international eventing, although national championships still went ahead.

The European Championships of 1969 were held at Haras du Pin in Normandy, the home of one of the French National Studs. This event did one good thing in that it showed how well a horse will jump a big fence provided that it is solidly built. The use of hardwood for the top rails of fences was and still is an expense that other countries do not lightly undertake, but this was the material most freely available in the area. At this event, a new type of fence came into use, the Normandy bank, soon copied at every major event, but here being rather more natural. A jump onto a bank was followed, on the bounce, by a post-and-rails that formed the far edge. A horse therefore had to jump up before contending with quite a big drop. The steeplechase course here was typically French, several of the obstacles having quite heavy timber in them, and the water-jump lacking water.

This event was notable for the problem of crowd-control. At many fences there were several hundred people within the penalty zones. The regular equestrian photographers, of all nationalities, became more than a trifle frustrated, when having found safe sites to work from, they had a score of spectators come in front of them. When fences are in the natural line of country, and not 'island' fences, then some means of letting the public past must be provided. This same problem bedevilled the World Championships at Punchestown, Ireland, in 1970 even more, when spectators churned up the approaches to many fences during heavy rain. Both these events had far more spectators than had been expected by the organizers and in recent years it has been a problem capably tackled. Some events, noticeably the German ones, have recently gone to the other extreme, with plastic fencing to keep spectators well back, or even from crossing the course. When a course loops so that it is possible to see one horse at a number of fences, as in Haras du Pin, then the need for good crowd-control becomes more vital.

Mary Gordon-Watson, competing as an individual for Britain on her father's Cornishman V, emerged triumphant, to show that a mere slip of a girl could do as well

Above
Adjutant Fauré clearing a fence
at Saumur, home of the
renowned Cavalry School, on
Verdo

on this horse as Richard Meade did in Mexico. Anyone who has ever carried Mary's saddle and weightcloth only volunteers to do it once, unless a close friend. The same can be said of some of the other girls who add so much charm to the event scene. Richard Walker, who had won the Junior European title the year previously, in Craon, and Badminton that spring, with Pasha, took the silver medal and Bernd Messman on Windspiel the bronze for West Germany. Russia and West Germany followed Britain in the team awards.

With an ex-junior doing so well in Normandy it is perhaps time to talk about the Junior European Championships, as they have undoubtedly created a lot of interest in the sport, and brought many good young riders into international prominence. They were first held at Eridge Park in the South of England in August 1967. Many countries, having heard of the abilities of the British Pony Club, stayed away, and in the end only the French turned up. To make matters more interesting a team of British girls took on a British boys' team and the French team. This was a completely unofficial contest, but the French team won and this encouraged others to appear at Craon in 1968. Alain

Souchon with Roi d'Asturie received the distinction of becoming the first individual title winner.

The French won the first official team title on their home ground, although Walker took the individual award. The year following at Euskirchen, not far from Aachen, the event was unsatisfactory, the course being designed, some said, to suit a local boy whose dressage ability was better than his cross country riding. The event at Holstebro in 1970 was still a little on the easy side, but at Wesel, on the Rhine, not far from the Dutch border, a very fair course was built in 1971. Amongst those competing in the British team that year was Lucinda Prior-Palmer on Be Fair. Two years later she was winning the Whitbread Trophy at Badminton with the same horse, and in 1975 this combination was successful in the senior European Championship in Luhmühlen. The British took both team and individual honours in Wesel, and at each holding of the Championships since then they have taken one or other title. But the French have given them quite a bit to think about over the years. Bernard Clement won the individual title at Eridge in 1972 with Quel Pich and Olivier Depagne did the same in 1976 with Bobineau at Siekkrug. This latter event, very well run by the German Federation, showed the advantage of running the Championships as an entity in their own right, rather than making them the appendage of a senior event. The publicity for the event was first class, bringing in as a result over 10,000 spectators on cross country day.

The autumn of 1970 saw a major Dutch championship event at Deurne, not far from Eindhoven. To fit the steeplechase course in was quite a problem, and it eventually was held through the rides of a pine wood. Cornering was not possible at speed, but it was still a good attempt at getting an event going. Michael Moffett, competing in his first international event, won on Demerara for Britain. The following year the event was moved to Boekelo, not far from Enschede, and it has remained there. It has grown in stature, and now it ranks second on the autumn European scene, behind only Burghley or the championships of the year. In 1976 it had 43 starters, compared with the 29 at Achselschwang in Southern Germany, the 39 at Luhmühlen in Northern Germany, and 34 at the Belgian event at Heide-Kalmthout, not far from Antwerp. A horse that will freely jump into, over, through and alongside water is required for this event, where the many drainage ditches and dykes are used in conjunction with fences. The Dutch event enthusiast is hampered by the fact that four different organizations run Dutch events, the biggest split being religious. The sport is gaining in popularity, however, and is helped in that the editor of *De Hoefslag*, the Dutch equestrian weekly, is an eventer.

In 1971 the European Championships were held at Burghley with seven nations participating. The West Germans sent only two individuals, preferring one of their own events and, later in the same year, an international at Munich-Riem as their try-out prior to the Olympics of 1972. Princess Anne on Doublet won the individual title and Russia and Ireland followed up Britain in the team event. For Munich-Riem there were eleven full teams, plus individuals from Denmark, France and Switzerland. The steeplechase course was the same as for the Olympics the following year, although the cross country was completely different. The course followed the standard pattern for a major German event, being in one big circuit. Surprisingly the lower rails on many fences were fixed, rather than being removable, as is now the case, in the event of accident. Lorna Sutherland was the winning individual for Britain with Peer Gynt, but

had not Mark Phillips crashed through the final show jumping fence and then fallen with Rock On, his would have been the victory. The East German team finished second to the British team there. They had taken part at Badminton a few years previously, and their showing this time led to their participating in the Olympics.

In 1972 there was a CCI at Colombier, near Neuchatel in Switzerland, which the Italians and the Swiss used for their final work-out before the Munich Olympics. The Swiss team in the unofficial contest won, with the third Italian team taking second place before a trio of British girls. This course was built on a Swiss Army training ground. It is still used for national events, but fences have to come down after use. This led to the uprights being placed in sunken drainpipes so that they could be removed. The other major Swiss event is at Frauenfeld, but there is not a lot of eventing in Switzerland, although an 'alpine' circuit of events in Austria, Switzerland, Bavaria and Northern Italy has recently been formed.

The Olympics in Munich saw the building of some very big fences, with quite a considerable frontage to them, giving a wide choice of approach. This same characteristic was evident at Luhmühlen three years later, where some fences were 30 metres broad. Birch was used for many of the fences, making the obstacles attractive, but its use for obstacles intended to last is not recommended, as it rots easily.

Before Kiev in 1973, a new event at Heide-Kalmthout, near Antwerp, attracted five

Above
Sue Hatherly and Harley, members of the winning British team, at the shooting stand fence on the cross country course at Luhmühlen in the 1975 European Horse Trials Championships

teams. This was a very well run event, but with the cross country course a little on the short side and very twisty, making it impossible to achieve the optimum time. The Poles, who over the years have appeared at various events, caused a surprise in defeating the French by 5.8 penalties. This event still exists, but it is the only one of any significance in Belgium. Strangely few Belgian riders bother to appear at Boekelo.

One fence in Kiev, the second, a big parallel approached down a gully, led to the British losing their hold on eventing. The Swedes, resuming an interest in eventing, failed to get one horse past this controversial obstacle. It was the West German team that won, from the Russians. Aleksandr Evdokimov on Jeger won the individual title for the home side.

For the World Championships of 1974 ten nations fielded full teams, the top 12 individuals coming from the United States, Britain, Ireland and Canada. The team and individual awards went to the U.S., the former by a margin of 170 penalties over the British. Top rider from the Continent was France's Thiery Touzaint who finished 13th with Ut Majeur.

The year 1975 saw the European Championships at Luhmühlen, where there were some first-class fences, and an organization to match. Ten nations took part with full teams, but only six teams survived all three phases. The Russians overtook Britain's all-girl team in the final showjumping due to the fall of Sue Hatherly and Harley going into a double. Lucinda Prior-Palmer gained the individual gold with Be Fair, and Princess Anne took the silver on Goodwill, form that sent the two to Montreal in 1976. One particularly good thing came from this event, which drew a very large crowd—it has become a regular international instead of being strictly a German affair. Now there are three major events in Germany, Luhmühlen, Achselschwang and (from 1977) Walldorf. The French have also opened their event at Haras du Pin, although they still have many that are confined to French riders. Seemingly, as in French flat racing, the trend is to keep the prize money at home whenever possible. The French insistence on competing with home-bred horses possibly justifies the restriction.

With more and more events being held in Europe, and the number of spectators and competitors continually going up, there seems to be no reason why this sport should not continue to inspire widespread, international enthusiasm.

SELECTION
AND TRAINING

Choosing and Training a Cross Country Horse
Frank Weldon

For most people, choosing the right horse for hunting, horse trials or any other cross country activity simply does not arise. It has to be the horse they have got because there is no hope of raising the money to buy anything else and anyhow they are very fond of him. Yet, far from being a handicap, this can be a positive advantage, because the way a horse turns out—his eventual success or failure—will depend very largely on the amount of intelligent effort put into his training and ultimately on how well you ride. It is often better to persevere with the devil you know than chance your arm with the devil you don't! In any case never assume that possessing another horse will provide an automatic passport to success.

However, if you are starting from the beginning, have grown out of your pony or are genuinely fed up with your present horse and can afford it, then you have to go shopping.

Undoubtedly the best way to set about buying any horse is to follow the recommendation of someone whose opinion you value, who knows the animal and your own form. That way, at least some of the uncertainty is resolved. Good horses are rarely difficult to sell by reputation, so their owners are less likely to go to the expense of advertising. It is usually the more moderate that tend to hang around, but that does not mean that perfectly genuine horses cannot be bought through the columns of widely read, reputable, specialist publications. Indeed because of the ready response more and more owners now advertise as well as letting their friends and neighbours know that their horse is for sale, so this is probably the main method by which horses change hands.

Some people are suspicious of dealers and there is no doubt that, if you are selling, a successful dealer will never give you a penny more than market value. Possibly a bit less, because he has his profit to think about. If you want to buy, though, there are many worse ways than taking advantage of a reputable dealer's skill and experience. Once again, you are unlikely to pay less than the horse is worth but it is not in the dealer's interest to sell you a pup. Except for bloodstock, auction sales are usually the last resort for sellers, so the inexperienced buyer would be wise to turn a deaf ear to stories of the bargains that have been picked up there and leave auctions to the experts, who know what they are doing.

Whatever method you choose and however well advised you are, you must eventually make up your own mind. No one else can do it for you and naturally what everyone is looking for is a good-looking horse, with no unpleasant habits—'good to box, clip, shoe and in traffic' as the advertisements go, well-mannered and fast enough to have no difficulty in keeping up with the others. Yet of all the many qualities required of a cross country horse, the most important is that he should jump and this, unfortunately, is not a gift possessed by every horse, however admirable he may be in every other way.

All horses can probably be *made* to jump, within certain modest limits and provided the conditions are ideal. The snag is, conditions rarely are and in the course of a day's hunting or a cross country round there is bound to come a time when even the best of riders will lose one rein or both irons and find himself sitting on the back arch of the saddle like a sack of potatoes. This is where a courageous, athletic horse will get him out of trouble, for the true cross country horse will, if need be, jump not because of, but in spite of the rider.

But how can you tell in advance if he possesses this enviable gift? The short answer is that you cannot and that is why those who can afford it go for horses which have proved themselves in the hunting-field, at horse trials or in showjumping. Such horses are inevitably more expensive because you must expect to pay for the time and skill that have been put into their training. They are not necessarily the best answer either, for you should always ask yourself why anyone should want to get rid of a horse that has done so well unless it has reached its ceiling, is difficult to keep sound or is a nuisance in some other way. Perhaps, also, you yourself may not be able to ride him quite as well.

A good showjumper may be ideal and several have distinguished themselves at horse trials, but be a bit wary of a novice showjumper being sold because he is thought unlikely to make the height in top-class competition. The fact that in horse trials he will never have to jump higher than 3ft 11in (1.20m)—well within Grade C limits—is beside the point. The take-off or landing at most cross country obstacles is rarely perfectly smooth and unless a horse has plenty of athletic ability in reserve, he will find them just as difficult as 5ft (1.50m) show jumps.

Probably the best bet for most people is for a four or five year old that has been backed and ridden for six months or so and has preferably had a few days' hunting. Much more will have to be taken on trust but at least you can ride him and should be better able to tell if he is likely to suit you than you can a green, unbroken youngster.

Whatever the age of the horse, his experience or lack of it, it is essential to study his conformation closely. It will certainly be impossible to say by looking at him if a horse is going to be brilliant across country, but you can often tell if he is *not* or if he is likely to spend more time off the road than in work. Some lucky people are born with an eye for a horse and seem to know instinctively what to look for. Others learn the hard way by bitter experience and disappointments; but all can learn and go on learning all their lives.

Assuming that you are one of the less fortunates, the first fact to face up to is that perfection is impossible to achieve. The best you can hope for is a horse with many good, few indifferent and no really bad points. Minor weakness in one department can be compensated for by strength in others, but 'the strength of a chain is the strength of its weakest link' and it is never safe to overlook one really radical weakness. Like anything else to do with riding, judging a horse's qualities cannot be learned from books and even if it could, it would need a volume to itself; so here is only a brief summary of some of the salient features to look for in a cross country horse.

Type

There is nothing a common horse can do that a well-bred horse will not do better. He does not have to be a racehorse, indeed it is probably preferable that he is not; but unless he has that indefinable stamp of class or breeding he is unlikely to have the stamina or guts to go on trying when things get difficult.

Size

In England a horse must be at least 15hh to compete in horse trials, but that is the only essential limitation, for there is no ideal height. Clearly a tall rider with long legs may feel out of place on a small horse, but Australian Bill Roycroft who is over 6ft won at Badminton on Our Solo, barely 15hh. On the other hand, very big horses are more likely to suffer the ills of the flesh than are their more compact brethren.

Sex

Most people prefer geldings because mares tend to be unreliable, even downright awkward, when they are in season, but this is certainly not true of all mares. A more recent example than Our Solo of an outstanding mare is Ballycor, on which Tad Coffin won the individual Three Day Event gold medal at the Montreal Olympics. The mares to steer clear of are those that seem to be frequently in season and any tail-swishing, laying-back of ears or tendency to squeal should be regarded with suspicion.

Colour

Colour is largely a matter of personal preference, but whatever it is, the shade should be strong rather than light. More important still, the colour should get darker towards the extremities. For instance, even a light, washy chestnut colour with darker legs and tail may be perfectly all right but a bay or brown that runs to mealy flanks and legs with a flaxen tail is a sign of a weak constitution.

Conformation

Probably the best time to examine a horse is when he is looking a bit poor. It may require more imagination to visualize what he could eventually look like and it is remarkable how his whole shape will improve when he is muscled-up in the right places. However, his muscular development will be largely determined by the boney frame and that does not alter.

'A head like a lady and a farewell like a cook' was the Victorian description, as expressed in polite society, of an ideal horse. A big, common head is a great disadvantage at the end of such a long lever like the neck. It is also ugly; and do not forget, that is what you are going to see most of, looking over the box door, in years to come. On the other hand, do not be over-impressed by a pretty, effeminate-looking head. Large, prominent, mild eyes set in a broad forehead enable a horse to see round

himself easily and to focus, and so help to make him fearless and confident; while small, sunken eyes restrict his vision and make him suspicious. Showing the white of an eye may not be very attractive but in my experience it is not a sign of viciousness or unreliability, as is generally supposed. Broad jaws, wide enough to take your clenched fist thrust up from below, tend to make it easier for the horse to flex at the poll.

A short, thick neck, especially when there is more muscular development on the underside than the top, certainly makes it more difficult for him to carry his head in the right place and should be avoided.

Prominent withers and a sloping shoulder make for a comfortable ride and enable a horse to raise his forelegs when jumping, while with low withers and a straight shoulder, the rider feels perched on the edge of a precipice.

Breadth of chest is obviously necessary to give room for vital organs like heart and lungs but vertical depth through the heart is even more important. I would worry less about a narrow forehand than a wedge-shaped body, tapering in depth from back to front.

Cannon bones suffer a lot of work and the shorter they are the stronger they will be.

Indeed the length of the foreleg between knee and fetlock should be considerably shorter than that from elbow to knee. Good bone is desirable in any horse but in the well-bred animal, great thickness is less important than prominent, flat joints, which provide the attachment for strong muscles, tendons and ligaments.

A long, hollow back will never be strong, however comfortable it is to sit on, and a horse that is narrow across his loins, looking as if he is short of a rib, will never be easy to keep in condition. On the other hand a reasonable length is essential for speed and with an excessively short back, the horse finds it difficult to get his hind legs underneath him.

As regards the *hind legs*, do not take the Victorian adage too literally and assume that an enormous backside is essential or even desirable. It is the proportions that count and seen from behind, the hips of a good cross country horse are likely to be quite narrow, but the quarters will then swell outwards as the eye drops down, with the second thigh most strongly developed. The longer the distance between the tail and the point of the hock the better, but the part of the leg below the hock cannot be too short.

Once again, the bones particularly of the hock joint should be large and prominent, to take well-developed muscles, tendons and ligaments which will provide most of the motive power.

The next stage is to see how the horse moves at walk and trot, when led in hand. Do not expect to see any exaggerated action, but you get a more critical view this way than if a skilful rider is covering some deficiency. A heavy, ponderous tread is obviously undesirable and the more the hind legs swing forward towards the forelegs, the more athletic the horse is likely to be. Any deviation from a straight line by either fore or hind legs is undesirable, whether they go too close together or too wide apart.

Always get the seller to ride the horse first, not just to prove that he will be safe for you to risk your neck on later, but to get an idea of how he may perform under ideal conditions. See how he moves at all paces and particularly at the faster ones, whether he lengthens his stride or just moves his legs quicker. The horse is bound to jump the obstacles happily on his home ground, chosen by the seller, and there is no guarantee that he will be equally confident with a different rider in strange surroundings. The best you can hope to get is an idea of his athletic ability. I would prefer a young horse to approach a small fence even a bit apprehensively and jump awkwardly, but then be content to pull a mouthful of grass, rather than one that sets off flat-out and jumps extravagantly, but then takes half a mile to pull up. Both are green but the latter is much more likely to dislike jumping.

The acid test comes when you ride the horse yourself, and it is remarkable how all pre-conceived notions can change—for the better or for the worse—as soon as you sit on the horse's back. Sometimes you are pleasantly surprised at the sense of power, strength and elastic movement in what appeared to be an unexciting horse, while a better-looking animal can give you a downright disappointing ride.

Whoever you are buying it from, it would be lunacy to clinch any deal without first having the horse examined by a veterinary surgeon, but his responsibility is only to express an opinion on the horse's soundness at the time. It is not his job to forecast if it will suit you or if it will still be going strong in five years' time, although an experienced vet can often say if it is safe to overlook some minor defect he has noted.

Do not be surprised if, when you get your new purchase home, you are not quite so enraptured as when you first saw him. You will be very lucky not to find some defect that you wish you had noticed before. However, if it is any consolation, of all the horses I have bought, the ones I was most depressed about early on often turned out best.

Training Scheme

It would be dangerous to try to suggest any rigid timetable of work to suit every horse. What you do will naturally depend on a horse's age, state of development and what he has been doing recently, but variety is the spice of life for horses just as it is for human beings. The secret of maintaining his interest, and keenness to learn, is to keep ringing the changes, and above all, not to persist at any activity beyond the stage when it becomes too physically demanding.

For instance it is better to split the day's work into two spells of 45 minutes, say one before breakfast and the other in the afternoon, rather than bring the horse in flagging after one 1½-hour session. Of course if you have to spend most of the day earning your living or looking after a family, this may be out of the question, but it is then all the more important to keep changing the routine when you *are* out.

It should only rarely be necessary for a horse to work hard for more than 1½ hours a day even when he is getting fit. Anything that cannot be learnt in that time is far better left to the next day, but that does not mean he should be shut up in isolation for the rest of the 24 hours. All horses enjoy human company and welcome a walk out, say for a bite of grass, whenever there is time.

However, horses are creatures of habit and can only learn through constant repetition, so in addition to catching them in the most receptive mood when they are fresh, it is not a bad thing to impress on the memory of an event horse that dressage comes first. They soon learn when they must be on their best behaviour without having to be exhausted first, so usually start with a spell of training on the flat.

If the horse is fat and soft or poor and weak off grass, the first training stint would be for only a few minutes long, to be followed by a quiet walk to relax and see the sights. Very soon a little jumping can be introduced to vary the monotony but only now and again should this first session 'in the gymnasium' be omitted because it is the very foundation on which everything else is built.

Training on the Flat

Volumes have been written on the art of riding and fascinating many of them are; valuable too, to compare notes with afterwards, but none are more helpful than a few practical lessons from a knowledgeable teacher who has the gift of being able to express himself in terms the rider can understand.

It would be a waste of time therefore in this chapter to do more than emphasize one basic principle which not everyone finds easy to understand—that whether you are riding a sluggish horse that skilfully avoids taking hold of the bit or one that always seems to be going 5mph faster than you would like, the remedy is the same—to make his hind legs more active. The more his hind legs come underneath him, to bear a greater proportion of both his own and the rider's weight, the lighter and more responsive he will become.

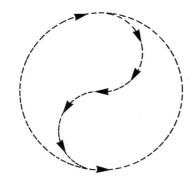

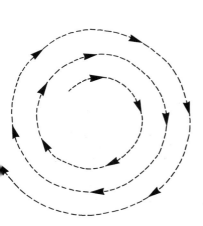

The main purpose of schooling on the flat, therefore, is to make the horse more responsive to the rider's leg and the distribution of his weight, for both are equally important, whether on accelerating or on slowing down. Of course the reins are indispensable, not only to indicate direction, but for their main purpose, which is to prevent all the energy generated by your leg from flowing out of the front end; the action of the reins however must never be divorced from the action of the legs. Right from the beginning, therefore, it is essential for the horse to regard the bit as an ally, not an enemy, and the milder it is, the better. A properly adjusted drop or grakle noseband can be helpful to keep the bit in the right place by discouraging the horse from opening its mouth, but that is all it can do. It has no other magical properties and can probably soon be dispensed with, even if it is first necessary at all.

The trot is the most suitable schooling pace as there is more natural momentum than at walk and it is less stimulating than canter. Indeed the canter should only be attempted when the trot is regular and confirmed, but do not get into the habit of only walking to give yourself and the horse a rest. He must also learn to walk out actively on the bit.

It is convenient to work in a circle to practise the correct bend, but, especially to start with, make the circle big and always resist any temptation to pull the head and neck round more than the curve of the body. The body, after all, bends very little so the head and neck should appear almost straight, with only the slightest curve to the direction in which he is travelling. All horses start by being stiffer on one side than the other and it is logical to concentrate on the stiff, but never persevere too long in one direction at a time. On the contrary, frequent changes of direction by means of the 'half figure-of-eight' help to accentuate the lesson and are a valuable suppling exercise.

Another useful exercise, to help make the horse responsive to the leg, is to start in a circle of fairly small diameter, say 15 yards, then, with the inside leg drawn slightly back, to ask him gradually to increase the diameter of the circle by means of the inside leg. This exercise can also usefully be performed at the walk.

Jumping

One of the most widely held misconceptions about jumping is that the faster you go, the easier it will be for the horse. Nothing could be farther from the truth. All horses, especially the less experienced, need as much time as possible to weigh up the problem and the main reason why horses stop is that their training has been hurried and they do not really understand how to organize their legs.

With a young horse, and even more with an older one that needs his confidence restoring, there is no better way of starting jumping than at a trot. Indeed if you have to start right from the beginning, it will be necessary to scatter a few poles on the ground at random and walk over them.

As soon as the horse is confident over these, he should be ready to tackle a few jumps during the normal training session on the flat. Ideally some low, inviting obstacles are scattered round the familiar field. Tree trunks are ideal, at varying heights up to about 2ft (60cm), but cavalletti or showjumping poles will serve. Do not attempt a series of obstacles, even a line of cavalletti, until the horse is jumping confidently over single fences. It is much better to vary the direction of approach, and circle left or right in between, and so take the opportunity to correct the trot, get the hind legs more active and achieve the correct bend. Only when the horse is paying attention and going forward properly is it time to consider the next jump, because the way he performs will depend almost entirely on the quality of the approach. When the pace, balance and impulsion of the approach are correct, a good jump will follow as a matter of course.

For this reason it is valueless to aim purposefully at a fence at a spanking trot—or any other pace for that matter—but then allow the horse to go slower as it gets closer, culminating in an almighty kick and, with any luck, a convulsive heave. On the contrary, start slowly enough to allow the horse to increase his length of stride as he approaches, but do not at this stage give him any signal to take off. If the approach is correct, he will be able to decide far better than you and will soon learn to take off from further and further away, of his own accord. In any case it is a good thing for him to learn to be self-reliant because later on, when jumping in earnest, even the best of riders can make a mistake.

Remember to keep contact with his mouth right up to the precise moment that he leaves the ground. It is only when he is in the air that he needs all the freedom you can give, but nothing is more likely to make him lose his balance and stop, than dropping his head in the last few strides. One final word of warning: make every effort to sit perfectly over any schooling jumps, and above all avoid getting left behind. It must be unpleasant enough for a horse to have to tow a rider over a fence by the reins, but even more uncomfortable to have his full weight landing with a bump on the part of his back least well-equipped to withstand the blow.

This is the usual cause of one fairly common phenomenon—the horse which scoots off as soon as he lands. He is trying to avoid the discomfort in the only way he understands and for this reason it is better to rise at the trot into any schooling fence, even though it is easier to create impulsion when you sit. Another common fault is rushing, often found in horses that have been spoilt by someone else!

To take a stronger hold in the approach is admirable, but the reason why horses hurl themselves headlong on being presented at an obstacle is not that they enjoy jumping but rather that they want to get the whole distasteful business over as quickly as possible. They are more likely to stop dead at the last minute anyhow. Such horses benefit enormously from a spell of trotting over simple fences, but how can you trot if the horse persists in loosing off as soon as he sees one? The answer is to turn into small jumps from only a few strides away, so as to give him no time to get up speed and take charge. With constant repetition, interspersed with calming circles at a trot, plus reward and flattery, it rarely takes a horse long to realize that jumping is less alarming than he thought.

Ditches

Many horses, even those which jump confidently over upright fences, seem to be unreasonably scared of any hole in the ground and, however illogical it may seem, it is essential to take a lot of trouble to allay their anxiety. Always start over the smallest ditch you can find and approach at the walk, or at the most a slow trot. He is bound to pause on the edge anyhow and jump it from a stand, even if he goes first time, so it does more harm than good to rush him at it. Hold him straight on the brink and politely but firmly encourage him to take the plunge. As with any jumping, it is essential to keep a firm contact with his mouth, although this is much more difficult when all forward movement ceases. Only turn round to try again if the horse succeeds in turning sideways, because it is surprising how long some take to pluck up courage. Be prepared to spend an hour at a time and return as often as necessary, but make things as easy as possible by aiming towards home or better still, towards his companions.

Only when the horse is jumping confidently from a walk over ditches several feet wide is it wise to attempt a faster approach and by then your troubles will probably be over for good.

Combinations

Even before the young horse has graduated to cantering over simple single fences, it is well worth introducing a combination of two or more obstacles close together. Trotting over a few cavalletti at 5-6ft (1.50-1.80m) intervals is a good start, and a valuable exercise is two cavalletti followed at 11-12ft (3.40-3.70m) by a small fence at two feet (60cm) high gradually increasing to three feet high, with a spread increasing to three feet wide.

The exact intervals will be determined by the horse's natural stride, but do not be tempted to reduce them too much. Instead, try to encourage a longer stride. 'Bounce' combinations, where the horse lands over the first element and takes off immediately for the second without a stride, are becoming a common feature of horse-trials courses. They are much easier for the horse than might be expected, and, provided the height is kept to about 2ft (60cm) with an interval of 13-14ft (4-4.30m) between, make an excellent gymnastic exercise at a trot. Any higher than that and the interval should be increased gradually to 15ft (4.60m).

Sooner or later in any horse-trials course there is bound to be a 'coffin' of some sort, which usually causes more trouble than any other type of obstacle. Few people find it

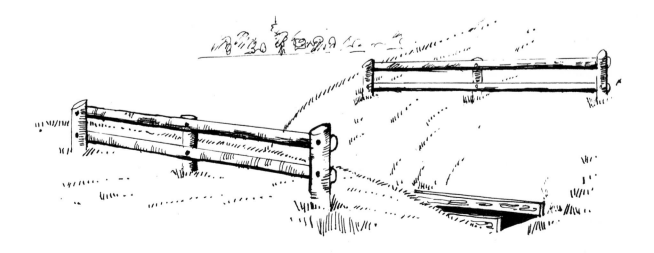

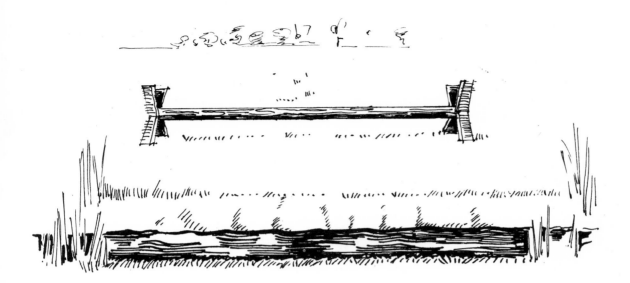

easy to represent such conditions at home, but the tricky part is persuading the horse to jump the first rail. Once over that, the ditch and the second rail usually follow without much difficulty, so if you can find a plain ditch, it is well worth putting a rail in front with which to practise. Even a cavalletti 10-12ft (3-3.70m) away will do, if there is no chance of erecting a more substantial rail. Jump the ditch by itself first, to reassure the horse before trotting energetically in to take both, one after the other.

Water

There remains one type of obstacle commonly met on the hunting-field or cross country course.

Jumping over water rarely presents much difficulty; indeed most horses seem to find it less alarming to jump a ditch brimful of water than when it is dry. On the other hand it is a great boost to the rider's morale to know that his horse is unlikely to object to getting his feet wet, if he has to go into water.

Some horses seem to love paddling and, if you do not watch out, they will get down and roll as well, but others will go to extreme lengths to avoid stepping in a puddle and it is well worth taking some trouble with these. If there is no suitable place to practise near home it may be necessary to go further afield. It is essential that the sides and bottom of the stream or pond are sound, because a boggy, spooky hole will do more harm than good. A ford is ideal because the approach is always gradual and the bottom firm. Once the horse is confidently splashing in and out, a cavalletti rail can be placed a few feet away from the bank for the horse to trot over first, and then it can be moved gradually closer until the horse eventually jumps in the water.

Further Training

How much further training can be carried out at home will clearly depend on the facilities available, but everyone should continue their horse's education on the flat

Above
Chris Collins on Centurian
safely negotiates a drop into
water at Boekelo in 1974,
keeping in touch but giving
his horse all the freedom he
needs

throughout his whole career. Horses (and riders) go on learning all their lives; this
process needs very little space and in any case need not be confined to a riding school or
manège. A lot can be done even on a quiet road and there are many worse places for
starting two-track work like leg-yielding, shoulder-in and half-pass. It is no
contradiction to say that the prolonged, parellel grass verges help the rider to keep the
horse straight and, if he is going towards home, there will be the added bonus of extra
impulsion and desire to move forwards, without which it is impossible to carry out such
movements correctly.

Basic jumping training is best done in private, however limited the resources, but
there soon comes a time when you will want to test the horse's progress in public, and
quite right too. Provided the groundwork has been thoroughly completed, more harm
than good can result from trying to keep him in cotton wool.

Even if the ultimate target is to compete at a major eventing championship, there
could be no better training than a judicious season's hunting. With any young or unfit
horse you will of course have to be strong-minded, restrict him at first to one day a
fortnight and go home after a couple of hours however well he is going or whatever
hounds are doing. Still, there is no reason why you should not enormously enjoy the best
cross country sport of all, even if there is some ulterior motive, and the horse will benefit
just as much.

At other times of the year, no opportunity should be missed to take part in any
competitive activity that is available, be it showjumping, hunter trials, dressage,
working hunter or even showing classes. No one in his right mind would advocate
pushing a young horse beyond his capabilities or asking him to take on anything before
he is ready, but the main reason why so many horse-trials competitors are preoccupied
with not upgrading their horses too quickly is that they tend to confine their attentions
only to horse trials. Showjumping is a specific part of an event horse's curriculum which
many riders neglect, but whatever the activity and however far removed it may seem
from his ultimate destiny, almost any competitive experience is invaluable for both
horse and rider.

Schooling Fences

Few people are lucky enough to have sufficient space at home, or enough natural obstacles, to prepare a horse completely for any eventuality that he may meet during a day's hunting or in a cross country course. In fact, all you need to do at home is to teach him the basic principles of jumping and once he fully understands them, it is remarkable how quickly he will learn to tackle strange and unusual fences 'in the heat of battle'.

However, in order to teach those basic principles it is essential to have at least two or three obstacles of some sort to school over. They need not be very elaborate or expensive, but with a little imagination, very serviceable practice fences can be set up with only the minimum of effort or professional skill.

As it is most readily available and durable, such fences will inevitably most frequently be constructed of timber (lumber) and the stouter it is, the more inviting the jump. An extreme example is a tree-trunk, as compared with showjumping poles. Because of its profile and solid appearance, even the most inexperienced horse will always make a conscious effort at a tree-trunk and will never touch it. On the other hand, thin, spindly rails at an equivalent height are apt to get scattered more often than not and then you have to get off to put them up again!

The width of a jump is another important factor because if it is too narrow, the horse's natural inclination will be to by-pass it rather than jump over. A width of 18ft (5.50m) is the ideal minimum for a schooling fence and if it is much less some form of 'wing' is advisable to help concentrate the horse's attention.

Of course, unless you have a suitable dead tree which is to be felled, massive tree-trunks, however admirable, may be out of the question. The cost of purchasing them elsewhere and transporting them to the right place could be prohibitive. Yet much smaller trees or big branches, 9-12in (27-36cm) in diameter, will serve almost as well. In order to achieve the required height, anything from 18in (46cm) to 3ft (60cm) or more, the log can be rested on criss-cross pieces of cord-wood as shown. It is remarkable what heavy weights can be raised, one end at a time, by means of a stout pole used as a lever, but if you want to avoid all physical effort, then a farm tractor with a fore-loader is the answer.

Once tree-trunks like this are in position, they are likely to stay there for good, but it is well worth also acquiring a few stout rails about 6in (15cm) in diameter and about 18ft (5.50 m) long. Although still heavy, they offer more scope for altering height or spread.

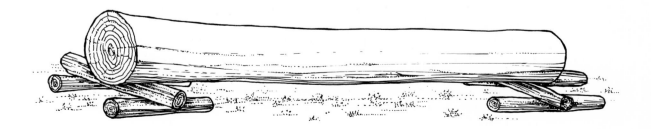

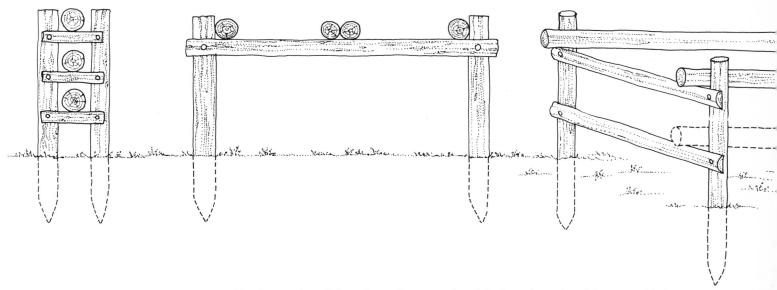

Fencing stakes driven into the ground, with short lengths of batten nailed across them, provide a convenient method of constructing an effective upright fence which can be adjusted for height.

In order to make a spread fence, the fencing stakes should be driven about 4ft (1.20m) apart and a short length of fencing rail nailed across them as shown to support the rails. However heavy the rails, they can easily be moved across the supports, providing for infinite variation in spread limited only by the distance apart of the two stakes. From here it is but a short step to combine the two ideas. The result is an easily adjustable obstacle, of which the profile can be varied from a straight upright fence to a true parallel with different heights and spreads. In each case, if the rails are stout and heavy enough, they will be anchored quite firmly enough by their own weight. Indeed if you want to avoid the risk of muddy breeches, it is preferable not to fix the rails any more firmly, so that there is some 'give' if the horse makes a bad mistake!

When set at a moderate height or spread, such an obstacle can conveniently be used in conjunction with cavalletti to introduce a horse to combinations, but it can also be constructed to provide a full-sized jump, say 3ft 9in (1.40m) high with a 4ft (1.20m) spread, when required.

A problem that frequently occurs with any permanent schooling fence which is used frequently is that the ground on each side gets cut up in wet weather. The solution is to spread liberally a material such as unwashed natural gravel. Although its appearance varies with the locality, this is essentially stone or gravel with clay mixed with it, as it comes out of the ground.

It is essential however to take two precautions. The first is to specify '$\frac{3}{4}$in gravel', which means that the diameter of the largest stones will not exceed $\frac{3}{4}$in (19mm). The second is not to spread it when the ground is already wet and muddy—if the gravel is spread a few inches deep while the ground is still fairly dry, a cheap and effective all-weather surface is produced, which can be used immediately. If you wait until there is a muddy bog, however much gravel is added the bog-like conditions will persist.

Picture acknowledgements

Permission to reproduce photographs has kindly been given by the following. (Page numbers in bold refer to colour illustrations.)

Howard O. Allen: 38. Skip Ball: 102. Eric Bryce: 132-3. Central Signal Photographic Laboratory, Chicago: 164. Alix Coleman: **106**, **175**. Gerry Cranham: **157**. Findlay Davidson: **53**, 97, 99, 190, 199, 213. Jerome Delcourt: 55, 56-7, 59, 188, 192, 195 (both), 196. Jack Dewell: 92, 166-7, 170, 173, 177, 179, 181, 182. Mary Evans Picture Library: 20, 52, 108 (top), 186 (both). Leigh Francis: 198. John Freeman Limited: 36. Photos Guilloux: 108 (bottom), 111, 114-15, 116, 120. Clive Hiles: 141. Hoofs and Horns, photo by K. Stevens: 176. Ray Horsnall: 24. Stanley Hurwitz: 29, 32. Leslie Lane: 134, 137, 151, 153, 154, 159, 161, 183. Douglas Lees: **18**, **35**, 41, 46 (both), 71, 82, 85, 86, 88-9, 91, 95 (both), **124**, **158**. Studio Léo: 113, 119. Nelson M. McClary: 44-5, 48, 49. Mansell Collection: 64. Marston Photographics: 144, 148-9. Jim Meads: 14, **17**, 19, 26, **123**, 125, 139. Desmond O'Neill: 202, 206. Roy Parker: 131. Bernard Parkin: 142. Mandy Reynolds: 146. Ruth Rogers: 6, 22, 128. Alec Russell: 73, 127. John Sedgwick: 58. George Selwyn: 2-3, 62, 65, 67, 68, **72**, 75, 77, 78, 80, **105**, 126, 129, 130, 216-17. John Taylor: 54. Reproduced from USCTA News, photo by Karl Leck: 172; photo by Joe Sekora: 169.

The drawings on page 211 and 212 are by Patricia A. Frost. Other drawings by Stuart Perry and Rosamund Pickless.

Note on currency conversions
Sterling–dollar equivalents are given at the rate of £1.00 = $1.71.
Francs are converted at the rate of £1.00 = 8.2f.

Previous page
Red Rum (left of picture) has his final gallop the day before the Grand National on Southport beach with a stable companion

Notes on contributors

PHILIP BLACKER became a professional jockey eight years ago after having ridden only six winners as an amateur. Before that he did showjumping. He has had 200 winners in all, 40 in one season, 1975/6. Besides being a jockey, he is a part-time sculptor, and has recently been making and selling bronzes of horses he has ridden, including Master H (12 winners).

MICHAEL CLAYTON has been Editor of *Horse and Hound*, the world's most authoritative weekly equestrian publication, since 1973. Before that he was a journalist in BBC television and radio, and on Fleet Street. He has been a lifelong horseman. He has hunted throughout Britain and the Irish Republic, visiting more than 40 hunting countries in a season in writing 'Foxford's' weekly hunting diary in *Horse and Hound*. He has written ten books on aspects of equestrian sports, and an anatomy of modern foxhunting, *A Hunting We Will Go*. He has commentated for BBC television at Hickstead, Badminton, and Burghley, among other broadcasting engagements.

CHRIS COLLINS was an amateur steeplechase jockey before turning to eventing. He came third in the 1965 Grand National and was Leading Amateur in 1965/6 and 1966/7, and in Europe has won the Swedish Grand National twice and the Grand Pardubice Steeplechase in Czechoslovakia (described in his article). He was a member of the British team in the World Championships Three Day Event at Burghley in 1974, and has been placed at Badminton and other international events. Apart from his equestrian interests,

he has had an active business career in the family perfumery firm of Goya. He is married to international event rider, the former Susanne Lumb.

FINDLAY DAVIDSON is a well-known freelance equestrian photojournalist. He has covered Three Day Events in seven European countries.

IVOR HERBERT is a bestselling author (15 books), has been a columnist on a number of national papers and was a successful racehorse trainer. He writes about personalities, travel, horses and racing in various papers including the *Sunday Express*. *Arkle* (1966; republished 1975), *Winter's Tale: study of a stable* (1974) and *Red Rum: story of a horse of courage* (1974; reprinted twice in 1977) head the list of his horse-writing achievements. In 1976 he made the controversial TV documentary 'Odds Against?' Apart from the paperback editions of *Red Rum*, he has three books being published in 1977, including his latest novel *The Filly*, published by Heinemann, and a study of steeplechasing stables, *Six at the Top*. He is published in France as well as in Britain and America. He deals in potential steeplechasers at his home in the Chilterns.

JANE KIDD has showjumped with international success and as a member of junior and adult British teams. She now specializes in dressage but enjoys hunting and riding out racehorses. Her books have included most recently *Horsemanship in Europe* and *Drag Hunting*. She was the compiler of the *Complete Horse Encyclopaedia* and the *Manual of the Horse* and was Assistant Editor of the partwork *The Horse*. She contributes to *Horse and Hound, Pacemaker, The Field, Riding* and *Chronicle of the Horse*. She helps run the family stud farm in Surrey.

JANE McILVAINE McCLARY is the author of fifteen books including *To Win the Hunt: a Virginia Foxhunter in Ireland, The Will to Win*, the story of Tommy Smith and Jay Trump's all-American triumph in the 1965 Grand National, and the recent international bestseller *A Portion for Foxes*. She has hunted with 82 packs in America, England and Ireland and written many articles on hunting and chasing for publications at home and abroad. She lives in Middleburg, Virginia.

ANNE MARTIN is the equestrian correspondent of the London *Evening Standard* and the *Birmingham Post*. She writes regularly for *Horse and Hound* and *The Field*, has broadcast for the BBC for fifteen years, and has had many successes in the show ring herself. She is married and lives in Warwickshire.

JOHN OAKSEY is the racing correspondent of *Horse and Hound*, the *Sunday Telegraph* and the *Daily Telegraph* as well as a racing commentator for Independent Television. He was co-author of *The History of Steeplechasing* and wrote the classic horse biography *The Story of Mill Reef* (1973). As John Lawrence Lord Oaksey was one of the most distinguished post-war amateur riders over fences. He retired in 1975 after twenty years as an amateur jockey, riding more than 200 winners and riding Corrickbeg into second place in the Grand National. He is married, with two children, and lives in Wiltshire. His wife Victoria is Field Master of the Vale of the White Horse Hunt.

SALLY O'CONNOR is an active competitor in dressage and combined training events. She was a founding member of both the Potomac Valley Dressage Association, of which she was President for three years, and the United States Dressage Federation. She is a freelance writer and has had articles published in *The Chronicle, Horse Play, The Maryland Horse,* and *Dressage*. She serves on the Advisory Board of the United States Combined Training Association and acts as its public relations officer. With four horses currently in training, Mrs O'Connor still takes time to officiate as a recognized judge at dressage shows throughout the country and helps instruct the Learner Judges Programs initiated in the past three years. At present she has a book in manuscript containing an account of an epic ride she made in 1973 with her two sons, aged 13 and 11, from one side of the American continent to the other, from Maryland to Oregon.

JOHN SEDGWICK started his hunting career at the age of two-and-a-half, by being blooded after seeing a short part of a good run with the High Peak Harriers from a basket on a Shetland pony; all this following a meet at the Bull i'Thorn Inn. Since then he has done as much hunting of all sorts as he could. At one time he was a supernumerary whip with the Old Berkeley Beagles, he has followed otterhounds and staghounds, and for a good many years he hunted with the South Oxfordshire Foxhounds and then with the Vale of Aylesbury Hunt. He now lives near St Malo in France and as well as sailing still manages to be involved with horses and hounds.

FRANK WELDON, M.V.O., M.B.E., M.C., has been the renowned Director and course-designer of Badminton since 1964. The first forty years of his lifetime with horses were almost entirely devoted to point-to-points and steeplechasing. He rode the first winner under National Hunt rules at Haydock in 1936 and the last at Sandown in 1957. He started eventing at an age most people stop and in his first Olympic Games at Stockholm in 1956 aged 43 he brought home a team gold and an individual bronze. He has twice been winner of the Badminton Three Day Event and captained the British Three Day Event Team from 1954 to 1964. He is equestrian correspondent of the *Sunday Telegraph* and eventing correspondent of *Horse and Hound*.

Index

Pages numbers in italics refer to illustrations